ANIMAL SPIRITS HAVE ALWAYS BEEN WITH US. WE SIMPLY NEED TO UNDERSTAND THEIR MESSAGES.

Deer are good powers and can be messengers in many different ways. They can be our eyes and ears if we acquire their power. They can tell us what is up ahead on the road while traveling, help us see the future via dreams and meditation, and remind us that we should live lives that are balanced and graceful. If a woman sees a buck while traveling, it is a sign that she might soon meet a man.

Woodpeckers are symbols of wealth, good luck, happiness, and healing. If you hear or see a woodpecker pecking in a tree near your house, clap your hands three times, make a wish, and thank him for his message. He is a sign that money or a gift is coming your way. If someone is sick, the woodpecker is a sign that that person will get well.

Ants represent strength, intelligence, psychic ability, sharp thinking, and planning. Red biting ants are bad power and challengers. Other kinds of ants can be messengers and allies. Small ants are a nuisance.

LEARN THEIR MEANING, THEIR RITUALS, AND THEIR IMPORTANCE IN OUR LIVES . . . THE SPIRITS OF THE EARTH

BOBBY LAKE-THOM is a healer who has been schooled in both Western and Native American traditions. Of Karuk, Seneca, and Cherokee descent, he has taught and lectured extensively across the United States for more than three decades and is the author of two previous books on Native American culture and spirituality. He lives in Fort Jones, California.

Spirits
of the Earth

A Guide to Native American
Nature Symbols, Stories,
and Ceremonies

Bobby Lake-Thom
Medicine Grizzly Bear

A PLUME BOOK

PLUME
Published by the Penguin Group
Penguin Group (USA) Inc., 375 Hudson Street, New York, New York 10014, U.S.A.
Penguin Group (Canada), 90 Eglinton Avenue East, Suite 700, Toronto, Ontario, Canada
M4P 2Y3 (a division of Pearson Penguin Canada Inc.)
Penguin Books Ltd., 80 Strand, London WC2R 0RL, England
Penguin Ireland, 25 St. Stephen's Green, Dublin 2, Ireland (a division of Penguin Books Ltd.)
Penguin Group (Australia), 250 Camberwell Road, Camberwell, Victoria 3124, Australia
(a division of Pearson Australia Group Pty. Ltd.)
Penguin Books India Pvt. Ltd., 11 Community Centre, Panchsheel Park,
New Delhi – 110 017, India
Penguin Group (NZ), 67 Apollo Drive, Rosedale, North Shore 0632, New Zealand
(a division of Pearson New Zealand Ltd.)
Penguin Books (South Africa) (Pty.) Ltd., 24 Sturdee Avenue, Rosebank, Johannesburg
2196, South Africa

Penguin Books Ltd., Registered Offices: 80 Strand, London WC2R 0RL, England

First published by Plume, a member of Penguin Group (USA) Inc.

First Printing, August, 1997
36 35 34 33 32 31

Copyright © Bobby Lake-Thom, 1997
Line illustrations copyright © J. Guadalupe Gonzalez Diaz, 1997
All rights reserved

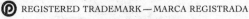 REGISTERED TRADEMARK—MARCA REGISTRADA

LIBRARY OF CONGRESS CATALOGING-IN-PUBLICATION DATA:

Lake-Thom, Bobby.
Spirits of the earth : a guide to Native American nature symbols, stories, and ceremonies /
Bobby Lake-Thom, Medicine Grizzly Bear.
p.   cm.
Includes index.
ISBN 0-452-27650-0
1. Indians of North America—Folklore.   2. Nature—Folklore.   3. Indians of North
America—Rites and ceremonies.   4. Indians of North America—Religion.   5. Tales—
North America.
E98.F6L25   1997   97-11026
398'.08997—dc21   CIP

Printed in the United States of America
Set in Cochin
Designed by Jesse Cohen

BOOKS ARE AVAILABLE AT QUANTITY DISCOUNTS WHEN USED TO PROMOTE PRODUCTS OR
SERVICES. FOR INFORMATION PLEASE WRITE TO PREMIUM MARKETING DIVISION, PENGUIN
BOOKS USA INC., 375 HUDSON STREET, NEW YORK, NEW YORK 10014.

DEDICATION

▼▼▼

This book, and its knowledge, is dedicated to my children, my nephews and nieces, my future grandchildren and great-grandchildren; to all the Indian children in my tribe; and to all those who are searching for a better understanding of this Earth, Nature, and spirituality.

It is also dedicated to the many different tribal elders who took the time in their lives to teach me so much; their spirit will always be with me, and in our prayers, ceremonies, and traditional Native rituals.

I would like to thank my literary agent, Sharon Jarvis at Toad Hall, Inc., for her encouragement and professional support in getting a publisher. I would like to thank Richard Adams, in Redwood City, California, for his assistance in editing and typing the manuscript. And I am grateful to Lupe Gonzales and his wife, Lena Case, for providing the artwork.

ACKNOWLEDGMENTS

▼▼

Instead of acknowledging anthropologists who may have recorded similar stories, I would like to recognize and thank the following Native American people and elders for being so kind as to share their stories and experiences for this book at community gatherings, and with the general public. This knowledge already belongs to the Native people and with their permission is being shared with others.

Seeley Griffin	Yurok Elder
Chuck Donahue	Karuk/Hupa Ritual Performer
Ed Chiloquin	Klamath/Modoc Elder
Jerry Roybal	Apache-Native American Consultant
David Shaw	Apache-Vet's Upward Bound Project
Frank Douglas	Yurok Elder
Charlie Thom	Karuk Medicine Man/Ceremonial Leader
Beeman Logan	Seneca Chief
Beverly Donahue	Karuk Elder
Raymond Legu	Pitt River Elder/Hereditary Leader
Shan Davis	Karuk Ceremonial Leader
Lottie Beck	Karuk Elder
Madeline Davis	Karuk Elder
Martin High Bear	Lakota Medicine Man/Sun Dance Chief
Darryl Wilson	Pit River Leader
Tony Gali	Pit River Traditionalist
Brown Bear J. P. Mallet	Tlinget Medicine Man
Glen Raymond	Colville Indian Educator
Isadore Tom	Lummi Medicine Man/Elder
Tony Mathais	Flathead/Kootenai Medicine Man/Elder
Raymond Many Bears	Blood/Blackfeet Medicine Man
Gilbert Brady	Northern Cheyenne Sun Dance Chief
Calvin Rube	Yurok Indian Doctor/Ceremonial Leader
Frank Kanawha Lake	Indian Student (Karuk)
Mandy Moccasin	Indian Student (Crow)
Willy Colegrove	Hupa Tribal Chairman/Traditionalist
Francis Brown	Arapaho/Shoshone Elder (Medicine Wheel Coalition President)
Bill Tall Bull	Northern Cheyenne Elder
Art McConville	Warm Springs/Storyteller
Flora Jones	Wintun Indian Doctor/Elder
Dewey George	Yurok Ceremonial Leader/Elder
Albert James	Wiyot Elder

CONTENTS

▼▼

A Native Prayer

O Great Creator,
I come before you in a humble manner
and offer you this sacred pipe.
With tears in my eyes and an ancient song from my heart
I pray.

To the four powers of Creation,
To the Grandfather Sun,
To the Grandmother Moon,
To the Mother Earth,
And to my ancestors.

I pray for my relations in Nature,
All those who walk, crawl, fly, and swim,
Seen and unseen,
To the good spirits that exist in every part of Creation.

I ask that you bless our elders and children, families and friends,
And the brothers and sisters who are in prison.
I pray for the ones who are sick on drugs and alcohol
And for those who are now homeless and forlorn.
I also pray for peace among the four races of humankind.

May there be good health and healing for this Earth,
May there be Beauty above me,
May there be Beauty below me,
May there be Beauty in me,
May there be Beauty all around me.
I ask that this world be filled with Peace, Love, and Beauty.

—Medicine Grizzly Bear
Earth Healing Ceremony
Spokane, Washington, 1990

Introduction

The following material can be very confusing and difficult to explain to those who have not been raised in the Native American culture, and without some guidance by a mentor. The authenticity may be questioned because it deals with a form of reality that is open to interpretation. Native American cultures are based on different perceptions and experiences with reality. Symbols, meanings, and omens—the communications with the Owl, Hawk, Spider, or Snake, for example—might mean different things to different people from different cultures or beliefs, or from different systems of thinking, from differences in imagination, or from different experiences and degrees of spiritual development.

Nature can and does communicate to us humans. Within this communication via omens, signs, and mythic-religious symbols is a definite system of knowledge. Until recently this knowledge was primarily reserved for medicine men or medicine women, or what Western people call shamans, who traditionally hoarded it for themselves or occasionally shared it with their people. Consequently, not all Native American people will know about this system of knowledge, but those who have been raised in the "traditional" Native American cultural ways will have some understanding and appreciation of it.

By the same token, I want the reader to realize that the unique knowledge shared in this book is not meant to represent all Native people and tribes. Nor should it be considered a romanticism of Native spirituality. It is simply this: *an opportunity to learn how to understand and speak Nature's language.* It is a rare opportunity for modern people to reestablish and reconnect with their relationship with Nature; to develop a real kinship with the Mother Earth, Nature, and *"all our relations"* in the Universe. It doesn't matter what race or nationality you are, or what religious belief you subscribe to; all that is required here is an open mind and a willingness to learn.

We are all part of Nature, we are all the Great Creator's children. So although the information shared here is from a traditional Native American healer, although it originates from Native American philosophy and ideology and is supported by Native mythology, it should not be construed as being representative of all Native American tribal or personal beliefs, knowledge, and practices. The Native American perspective and experiences being shared here are intended to help increase understanding, to bridge cultural differences, yet also to highlight similarities. I am sure that upon further research and comparison you will discover that the traditional cultures in Africa, Australia, Asia, and among certain groups throughout Europe and the Mideast might have a similar system of knowledge. Remnants of Western knowledge about Nature can be found recorded in ancient European myths, fairy tales, legends, and stories if the reader desires further comparison and study.

Despite both the positive and negative advances of Western

society and its impact upon traditional Native cultures, we just can't ignore certain forms of knowledge that have stood the test of time. We also can't ignore certain supernatural and mystical encounters that some modern people experience today. Some things that occur in Nature that affect our lives cannot be explained or verified by the rational mind, the academic intellect, or the scientific approach, or by religious precept or typical Western thinking. The more sensitive, curious, and liberal-minded are really caught in a dilemma. When something strange happens to them they can't understand, they call it "supernatural." If they begin to understand it and start to believe in it, others will say they are "superstitious." This conflict between rational and intuitive thinking is still being debated by some of the greatest philosophers in the world, while psychologists, psychiatrists, and scientists are constantly trying to establish new classifications to either hide it, suppress it, or figure out some way to logically explain it.

Things such as strange encounters with omens, signs, and so-called supernatural contacts with talking animals, birds, fish, bugs, lizards, snakes, clouds, winds, ghosts, or spirits seem like a foreign world to most modern people. And yet these things do indeed exist, whether as figments of our imagination or as actual realities making physical and sensory contact.

A couple of years ago I lectured at the Theosophical Society in Wheaton, Illinois, on the topic of "Native American Mythology, Symbolism, and Spirituality." I was talking about Nature and why we traditional Indians consider it sacred; how Nature is a teacher and healer to us; and why we believe it communicates through a system of symbols. At the very start of my lecture I did a prayer ritual, according to custom, as an acknowledgment of respect to the ancestral spirits and Nature spirits of that region. I burned some sweet grass and tobacco as an invocation, said a short prayer in my Native language, and opened with an ancient song. Within a matter of minutes a large

Raven flew in and landed on the open windowsill on the right, a Red-Shafted Flickerbird flew in at the same moment and landed on an open windowsill on the left, and lightning and thunder cracked immediately overhead several times on a perfectly clear day. Approximately 150 people were in attendance and saw this occur. Such an act is not "magic." It may be synchronistic, it may be spiritual, it may even be mystical, but it was definitely a demonstration of Nature communicating to all of us symbolically. And it was definitely a reality for everyone there who saw it.

The Raven hollered loudly, the Flickerbird whistled loudly. Both had gone out of their way to show themselves to all of us there, and the natural forces above us outside, hidden by the large building, made themselves apparent. Why?

I started my lecture in a dramatic way, seizing upon this unusual opportunity to lead into the discussion, which in turn served to provide the audience with an example of the phenomenon being discussed, not simply as a theory but as a reality. Was all this simply coincidence? I don't think so. But I am sure someone could rationalize it as an example of collective hallucination, mass hypnosis, or some other state.

So what does one in Western society do when encountering such phenomena? Who can you turn to for an explanation? Is it simply a coincidence when a small bird slams into the front room window of the house, or suddenly flies into the house, and shortly afterward a relative dies? Why just your house, and not the neighbor's? Why did a Snake suddenly appear next to you while you were sitting on the lawn at lunch break with some friends or colleagues. Why didn't it slide up to someone else instead of you, as if to say, "Hey, cousin, I want your attention here a minute"? Why did the Butterfly land on your shoulder when you were on your way to work, and not your friend's? What was it trying to tell you? Why did the Spider jump on your supervisor at

work, and not you? Why did the Hawk fly in front of your car and not cars in the other lane as you were coming home from work? Why did you see that furry animal by the road, and other people with you didn't even notice it? And what did it mean?

How many times do you actually see a so-called wild creature suddenly appear next to you in a city park, on the freeway, on a country road, or near your house no matter where you live? And what would you think if a big buck suddenly walked into your house, as happened to one man who attended my lecture? Was this simply a coincidence, or did it mean something? If so, what did it mean?

Perhaps it doesn't really matter what your belief system is and it doesn't matter how acculturated, assimilated, or educated you have become because you are still a primitive being with an ancient soul deep down inside. And it doesn't matter how urbanized the world becomes, because you are still living in Nature. It may be painted over, constructed over, polluted, or even obscured by Western modernization and thinking, but Nature is still there. Spiders and Toads can be found in sterilized hospitals. Falcons fly among city skyscrapers. Coyotes steal dog food from urban dwellers' back porches. A large Moose runs down a busy city street. A Snake appears near the altar of a local church. Thousands of Grasshoppers suddenly converge upon a small town in the country. A Whale swims up the Sacramento River and won't leave. A Great White Shark is caught five miles up a freshwater river. An Owl keeps hooting around your house every night at the same time.

It doesn't matter whether you live in Chicago, New York, or Los Angeles; in the country near Bristol, along the coast by Ocean City, in the wheat fields outside Spokane, near the cornfields of Topeka, in the desert of Elko, or on the plains of Billings. Nature is always there, communicating inside and outside of your perceptions. You don't have to go out into the so-called wilderness to encounter the phenomena;

sometimes the wilderness comes to you. And when it does come, some people just aren't prepared to accept it, so they either try to ignore it, dismiss an incident as simply a coincidence, or begin to consider Nature an enemy instead of an ally. They don't understand Nature's messages. What people don't understand they fear. Rather than trying to live with it, they try to conquer or eliminate it. Sometimes man destroys nature out of anger and frustration, and sometimes by deliberate intent. All those who walk, crawl, fly, swim, seen or unseen, who live among us in Nature, who are our "relations," are often treated as alien beings.

What I am trying to share here is my own interpretation and understanding of Native American knowledge as I have come to learn it and apply it. I learned it from the different elderly medicine men and women who trained me. I learned it from spending time with our Native elders and listening to the ancient "Grandfather stories." I learned it as part of my many years of training as a shamanistic doctor. As I learned more about the traditions, I became more aware, and more sensitive to them, and spent more time bonding with Nature.

There are a lot of people who honestly respect Nature, who want to love and care for Nature, and who would like to learn how to bond more with Nature or to heal their relationship with Nature. In order to learn how Nature actually communicates, however, we can turn to the traditional Native American people, elders, and healers for guidance, to Native mythology for teachings, and to some form of ritualization in order to gain experience. It is with this in mind that I have decided to share the following material. As a traditional Native healer, and because I truly believe in the value of Nature, I feel an urgency to disclose this material. If things in society get to the extreme that Nature can no longer communicate to us, or if it gets to the point that we, as human beings, can no longer recognize and understand symbolic communication, then we will no longer thrive as a species.

A Spiritual Understanding About Nature

I believe Nature communicates to all people. Maybe not all the time but at least some of the time. It appears, however, that most people are not aware of this communication going on around them. Some who notice it either don't believe it or they don't understand it. Profound encounters and messages are considered supernatural. Natural signs and omens are considered superstitions, and direct experiences are labeled hallucinations. Are we to believe that Nature itself is not real? Or have we just lost touch with the true reality?

When the first Europeans came to this country, they saw our Native American people praying to the Sun, Moon, Stars, Rivers, and Lakes; to the Trees and Plants; to the Wind, Lightning, and Thunder; and even to the Birds, Animals, Fish, Snakes, and Rocks. They called us pagans, heathens, and savages. For some strange reason they developed the idea that we did not believe in God, although in many different tribal languages there were references to a Great Spirit, the Great Creator, the Maker, the Great Mystery, or the Great Invisible One. The truth is that not only did the American Indians worship God, but they also respected and communicated with that which God had created.

Despite the forces of acculturation, traditional Native American Indians and the medicine men/women still understand the sacredness of Nature. They see the life-giving force of the Great Spirit flowing through all things in the Universe. Because of ancient beliefs,

teachings, and spiritual practices, they feel and maintain a direct kinship with all of Creation. According to traditional Native American belief systems, everything is a source of "power," and as a result it should be revered. The traditional Native American believes that each living thing in Nature has a spirit of its own, in addition to being connected to and part of the Great Spirit. That is why we pray and give thanks to the Sun, Moon, Stars, Rain, Wind, Waters, and all those that walk, crawl, fly, and swim, both seen and unseen. We realize that we cannot survive or live without our "relations." We also realize that they cannot live without us; hence there is a reciprocal relationship.

Evidence of this belief system can be found in Native myths, legends, and stories. Here one can find reference to the animals and birds as "people." The Bear is our grandfather, Rattlesnake our aunt, Beaver our cousin, Eagle our uncle, Deer our sister, and Buffalo our brother. But in a deeper sense of ideology, they are not only our "relations" but are also considered our teachers, protectors, guardians, supernatural aids, and sources of power and knowledge. This is not romanticism, it is reality. I believe modern people can learn from this ancient reality if they are willing to be open-minded. There is a special kind of telepathic and symbolic understanding between the traditional Native American and his/her relations in nature. We communicate through praying, talking, singing, dancing, meditating, touching, smelling, and/or offering tobacco, herbal smoke, food, or some other gift to one of our relations. Since Nature's language is symbolic, it communicates back to us in a unique way, with natural symbols.

Let me give you an example. One time, when I was a young boy, I was sitting on a riverbank fishing with my grandfather. We saw a Fox suddenly come down the side of the bank toward her den. She stopped, lifted her head up to the wind, and sniffed around in a nervous way. She then ran into the den, picked up one of her pups, and took it to higher ground. The second time she came down, my grandfather started talking to her in his Native language. She stopped as if listening to him intently, and then whistled at him four times. She ran back into her den and grabbed a second pup, then carried it up over the riverbank to a new home she had made, quite some distance from the river's edge. At that point my grandfather turned to me and said: "Hurry up, get your gear and fish, and let's get back to the house. We've got a lot of work to do right away." So I did as I was told. When we returned, my grandfather instructed other members of the family to move the tractor, all farm equipment, and the livestock far away from the river's edge. In a serious and urgent tone of voice, Grandpa told my uncles and cousins to board up windows and secure the house, barn, and sheds. My grandmother and aunts assumed responsibility for preparing emergency food and materials. Within a few hours a very bad storm came. Winds and rain raged across the mountain range for hours. That evening the river flooded. A considerable number of our neighbors suffered damage to livestock and property, while we were safe.

For years I wondered how my grandfather knew a flood was coming. A lot of people were amazed at the so-called psychic premonitions and power he often demonstrated. Whether it was good news or bad news, a positive event or a negative situation, for some reason he always seemed to have a way of knowing before certain events would occur. My great-grandmother, Kitty Hawk, was like that too. When questioned, she would often say: "Oh, a little bird told me!"

Grandpa wasn't a medicine man but he did believe in the "old Indian ways." He didn't like to be called psychic because he said the knowledge was there for everyone. He usually gave credit for his knowledge to the "Indian stories" that had been told to him as a boy. He taught me a lot of these stories, some from his own tribal heritage and the stories he had heard from friends from other tribes. And my learning was expanded in later years, as I spent more time with elders

from different reservations across the continent. It was from this upbringing that I began to realize that Nature is constantly talking to us. Unfortunately, very few people ever take the time to listen, watch, or learn the ancient language system. In contemporary society, no one teaches our children Indian stories at home or in school. As a result, Nature is becoming foreign to people and the esoteric knowledge is being lost.

Grandpa eventually revealed the secret to me. He said the Fox had told him a flood was coming. She had warned him symbolically by her actions. The Fox knew by "instinct," a natural source of knowledge and power that the traditional Indian uses as part of his spiritual growth and development and which most Western people and more assimilated Native Americans are no longer aware of. Instinct, however, is a reality. It is also a natural system of communication between Nature and the species, the mind and the body. The communication might come in the form of a physical symbol, or it might be more intuitive, making itself known through language, appearing as a hunch, a feeling, or an inner voice in a dream or through a vision.

Many Western people consider such forms of natural knowledge mysterious, supernatural, or superstitious. They don't understand it and they fear it, and as a result they find ways to ignore or discredit it. The art of studying signs and omens, however, is an ancient form of knowledge that was used by all races of humankind at one time or another in the history of their evolution. Europeans, for example, studied certain signs in Nature to find out when to plant or harvest crops, when to hunt, when to make sea voyages, and even when to get married. Have you ever heard "Red sky in the morning, sailor take warning; red sky at night, sailor's delight"? Some of this ancient, Western knowledge can still be found in the *Farmer's Almanac* today. For traditional Native American shamans, natural knowledge has always been a reality and a natural part of their ideology and spirituality. And although communication with Nature is an ancient system of knowledge, it is not archaic because this knowledge is still relevant today. We should remember, too, that not all signs, messages, or omens are bad.

Here is another example of using ancient knowledge to approach a modern problem. A friend of mine is from the Colville Indian Reservation in Washington State. One day he came to Spokane to talk to me about some personal problems. He had been unemployed for quite some time, was without money, and was worried about debts. While we sat drinking coffee and talking, I reached over into the cabinet and brought out the sweet grass herb and a Raven wing. I told him a few stories about the Raven, about how hard the Raven's life is, but somehow the bird always seems to survive, to "make it" in life. According to our Native myths, the Raven can bring good luck, if one is willing to make prayers to the Raven and ask for his help. So we did a cleansing ritual with the sweet grass, made prayers to the Raven, and threw some food up on the roof for him. We heard a large squawk a few minutes later, and watched a big Raven fly up on the roof. I told my friend, who was staring in amazement: "See, sometimes it works, huh?" A few days later he called me, very excited. He said he'd seen a Raven flying toward his house with food in its mouth, and he wanted to know what it meant as a sign. I told him it was a good sign, that his prayers would be answered. I also told him that the Raven was symbolically showing him that a gift was coming to his home. Later that day he received an unexpected inheritance check in the mail. And as if that wasn't enough, he also received a new job offer.

Fact, fiction, or fantasy? Who knows how communication with Nature works or why. All I know is that in some situations it does work. Our tribal elders and Native myths and Indian stories teach us that it is perfectly natural to call upon "supernatural" aid when all other resources seem to fail us. We are taught that the Earth is full of

many different kinds of spirits and powers, both good and bad, positive and negative, physical and spiritual, seen and unseen. And some of these "powers" are even neutral. We are taught that the "powers" come in the form of natural forces and elements of Nature such as Lightning and Thunder, Wind and Clouds, Earthquake and Fire; and in the Animal people, Bird people, Fish people, Snake people, Bug people, Tree people, Plant people, and Rock people. In other words, every part of the Earth is a physical and spiritual source of power and energy that directly affects us, the *"Human people,"* because we also are an integral part of the great family in Creation.

In order for us to survive as a species, we must learn to identify the purpose, function, and symbolic meaning of these natural powers. We must learn how such powers actually influence and/or affect our lives. We are taught by our elders, and via myths and ritual, how to use these powers in an efficacious manner. So my friend was taught how to call upon the Raven as a spirit guide for assistance. In a similar fashion, a medicine man/woman will recite an ancient mythic prayer formula as a means of bringing thunderclouds and rain.

I can understand how most people in Western society would consider the concept and acts of signs and omens magical, but they are also real. I, too, have been educated in Western thinking. I have different master's degrees, and have been trained by Western education to think "logically." But I have been fortunate to have also been taught by Native elders in a cultural context, and in a cultural-spiritual way. Hence I have learned how to make the appropriate psychic switch and to think with both sides of my mind-brain complex. And I have learned that it is perfectly natural to call upon "supernatural aid" whenever I need help in my life. Whether that supernatural help is viewed as projection of my subconscious mind or exists as a separate reality does not really matter. What matters is the fact that it truly exists for me as reality, and I have been taught how to see and understand it. And I believe all people who want to learn can acquire the same kind of knowledge. Our survival as a species depends on whether we progress with intelligence, meaning "whole intelligence," or whether we continue to remain limited. Most people are never taught how to use the unconscious, the intuitive-spiritual side of the brain.

Let me share another incident. A few months ago, while I was washing dishes, a little Spider came traveling down her web right in front of my face. She stopped for a moment to get my attention, then proceeded to go down into the drain. At the same time, I had my hand on the garbage disposal switch. I removed my hand out of curiosity, and partly out of respect for the Spider, not out of fear. I stopped what I was doing to try to communicate with the Spider. I even talked to her directly in English. "Oh, hello, little sister. Why did you come to visit me, what are you trying to tell me?" Then all of a sudden she jumped up on the sink and watched me. Out of curiosity I reached down into the drain where she had come from, and found a broken glass that was hidden from my view. Now, if it wasn't for that little Spider, which most other people would probably have killed out of fright, I would have turned on the disposal and sent shards of glass flying everywhere. I could have been injured, and possibly scarred for life! So, as you can see, Nature is also in the city. It can be found in our own homes and houses, and even in apartments and professional buildings in city skyscrapers. Thus there is an opportunity for us to learn from Nature everywhere, if only we open our eyes and our minds.

The Native American people have been studying signs and omens for eons. They use their knowledge to predict weather changes, as part of strategic planning in housing construction, or for planning trips, ceremonies, and in the past for making war. They use it as a means of survival. Europeans had similar forms of knowledge. Some farmers in this country have retained it, perhaps because they live closer to Nature and depend upon Nature for survival, whereas the more educated and urban-oriented have lost their bond with Nature; and their thinking has become more left-brain-oriented. For example, those who depend upon Nature for subsistence and survival have learned that Deer mating early is a sign of an early winter. But did you know that you can also tell how harsh the winter will be by looking at the bark on trees; by how thick the hair is getting on horses or your pet dog? And we know that the sudden appearance of Robins and Flickerbirds dancing in a crazy, nervous way around the front yard is a sign that a storm is coming. The appearance of spots on the Sun, called Sun Dogs, is an omen of droughts and social eruptions. When Sharks and Porpoises suddenly start going up freshwater rivers, it is an indication that floods are forthcoming. When Sea Lions rush up on the beach, a tidal wave is forthcoming. The sudden appearance of small Flies in the house is a sign that rain is coming, or even possibly illness and disease. The presence of large Blowflies in the house is an indication that evil is stalking the family. The sudden appearance of other kinds of bugs in Nature, such as the Lady Bug, in large mass can forewarn us of hazardous fires. Even different kinds of clouds can be messengers, telling us that a tornado or a hurricane is coming. Rings around the Moon serve as a sign that rain is forthcoming; different-colored clouds partially blocking the Sun or Moon can serve to warn of a coming sandstorm. The obvious lack of visible clouds or the bright red color of certain clouds can also warn of droughts. And a bird suddenly flying into the house is a sign of illness or even death, unless you have the knowledge and power to recognize the omen and change the situation.

All of this information is directly related to human instinct. It is survival knowledge. We have a right to learn it, use it, and not be taught to be ashamed because we believe in it. A person can learn more about this kind of natural knowledge by studying ancient myths and their symbolic meanings and inner knowledge. Even scientists are beginning to study the behavior of snakes, bugs, animals, and birds, domestic and wild, as a means of predicting potential earthquakes and other natural disasters. We must move beyond the stereotype that such knowledge is simply superstitious and learn to seek out its deeper meanings.

How I Learned Nature's Language

There are ancient secrets and lessons hidden in Nature, and if you seek for guidance, you will discover the truth. In order to understand Nature you will need to learn its language, its spiritual and symbolic meanings. In the old days our elders taught us stories and secrets about Nature while singing winter songs around the lodge fire.

You may want to know how I have come to understand Nature's language. I have been taught and trained by over sixteen Native elders, medicine men/women, and religious leaders from different tribes since I was a child, who say I was chosen by the Great Creator and by destiny to become a traditional Native healer, ceremonial leader, and spiritual teacher for our people.

My father is Charles "Red Hawk" Thom from northwestern California. He is a full-blooded Karuk Indian and a hereditary medicine man, ceremonial leader, and spiritual teacher. My mother, Ruby Blankenship, is part Seneca and part Cherokee. Her Seneca relatives come from the Allegany, Tonawanda, and Buffalo areas of New York, and her Cherokee family is scattered in North Carolina, Tennessee, and West Virginia. My mother is part Caucasian, and was raised with both cultural backgrounds and influenced by the forces of acculturation and assimilation. My father, on the other hand, is very traditional and speaks his language fluently. My stepfather was Seneca and Oneida and part Caucasian. Unfortunately, he didn't know much about his heritage and culture because he was urbanized most of his life, and was plagued with alcoholism. So my upbringing was influenced by my cross-cultural and interracial background, but the cultural side was strengthened by learning under the elders most of my life. The elders were traditional Native ceremonial leaders and healers, or what anthropologists call shamans.

Let me use my father and his spiritual background to demonstrate how a traditional Indian develops a philosophy about Nature. My father has the name "Red Hawk" for a reason. That is his main power or what some New Agers call a "totem." He inherited that symbol, power, and spirit ally from his grandfather, who received it from spiritual training in the sacred high country that we call the Chimney Rock or Doctor Rock area. The Red-tailed Hawk has been with my father since he was a child. It watched over him and protected him. It talked to him in dreams. It visited him in visions during sweat-lodge ceremonies and during his different power quests. It told him secrets about Nature, spirits, and powers. It gave him a special song to sing, which he in turn uses for good luck in hunting, for protection, for dreaming, for his traditional religious ceremonies, for counseling others, and as a source of personal power.

The Red-tailed Hawk, therefore, became his personal connection to Nature. It serves as a personal "telephone line" between him and the Great Creator. It is his passport into the spirit world, and his symbol of authority. As a child, he often found Hawk feathers. Sometimes he would find a whole dead bird, and at other times people would give him parts of the bird. So that "symbol" which he inherited and which resided in his unconscious mind somehow manifested itself in the physical world and could be perceived by the five senses.

As a child, whenever my father became sad, depressed, or worried

about something in life, the Red-tailed Hawk would suddenly appear, scream at him, and circle overhead. It was as if the Hawk telepathically knew, no matter how many miles away it was. It came to his aid and made its appearance felt physically, symbolically, and spiritually. This gave him reinforcement, encouragement, and motivation to learn more about Nature's ways. As the Hawk flew higher into the sky, it conveyed many meanings to the sad, depressed, Indian child below. It helped to lift this child's spirit. It let the child know that he was not alone, that he was being watched, protected, and guided. In this sense, it was a spirit guardian from Nature and a special gift from the Great Creator.

Historically, Nature has always rewarded our young Indian people for their spiritual awareness and commitment to learn more about the world around them; it rewarded my father when he was young and learning, when he would find Hawk feathers and bird parts. Upon finding such gifts, my father would then take them to the elders and ask for instruction as to what the gifts meant, and how he should use the spiritual symbols. Over the years he began to learn that the feathers were a confirmation of his power; they became the tools of his trade and symbols of the sacred profession he was destined to inherit. My father is an example of how a young shaman begins to learn Nature's language.

This special connection with Nature and this natural gift that serves as a unique source of power have saved his life many times. During his early manhood, my father, or Charlie, as his friends called him, worked as a lumberjack in the mountains. One day a forest fire got out of control and trapped his crew. They were surrounded by fire on all sides and in a state of panic. My father burned his angelica root and prayed to the Great Creator for help, for everyone's protection. Then he heard the scream of a Red-tailed Hawk flying in from the east; it circled and kept crying, and as it came down lower he could understand what it was saying "symbolically" and perhaps "telepathically." It said, "Follow me this way, hurry, gather everyone up, you can escape this way." And although he was burned quite badly and others in the crew were injured, they all managed to escape to safety and live because of Charlie's leadership during a crisis. To some outsiders or disbelievers, this example may seem like just a fabricated story, but to Charlie and his crew it was a reality and an experience worth remembering.

That Red-tailed Hawk is always near him, physically and spiritually. And I suspect it is even deep inside him because he has learned how to become one with it. Symbolically, it has become his "higher self." It doesn't matter whether he is in New York, Hawaii, Maryland, California, Nevada, or Montana. A Hawk always seems to appear to be following him. Whether he's on foot, traveling in a truck, sitting by the sweat lodge, eating in a restaurant, giving an indoor lecture, or just resting at home, it always seems to be somewhere nearby. Even when he was in the hospital and everyone thought he was dying, the Hawk came and sat on the windowsill. My wife Tela has the same gift, power, protection, and connection with Nature, whereas I have acquired the spirit guardians Raven and Crow. Leaders in the past such as Geronimo had the Sun and Coyote. Sitting Bull had the Buffalo. Crazy Horse had a sacred talking stone. Chief Joseph had Thunder and Clouds. Seatl had the Raven. Tecumseh had the Black Snake. The contemporary Native religious leader Wallace Black Elk has the Spotted Eagle (*The Lakota Sacred Way*).

I, too, inherited certain psychic gifts and spiritual forms of knowledge from my parents and foreparents. Strange things happened to me as a young child, in the same way they happened to my father. While I was in school, for example, Hummingbirds zoomed into my first-grade classroom and landed on my desk. A King Snake crawled up into my lunch bucket in front of my peers, a Butterfly landed on my ear. A flock of different birds suddenly swarmed around me in a soccer field. A Raven once defecated on my head in front of the elders! I talk about some of these personal experiences and encounters with power and death in my book *Native Healer*. For example, three different times I was pronounced clinically dead, but miraculously came back to life at the appearance of a Raven. In each situation the Raven was always symbolically and spiritually there for me.

I've had other kinds of strange encounters since I was a child, including encounters with Muskrats, Beavers, Otters, and Minks that went out of their way to visit and play with me when I was fishing with my friends. Spiders have jumped on me, Scorpions have stung me, and I have been attacked by a swarm of Bees. A Rayfish stabbed me in the foot while I was swimming in the ocean. A pack of Foxes attacked and chased me while I was visiting a cousin at his farm. Many times Deer and Elk have come right up to my face unexpectedly. On other occasions little Bluebirds and Wrens have landed on my shoulders. Grouse and Quail walk in front of me and alongside me while I am jogging. Many times in my life I have had large birds such as Hawks, Eagles, Ospreys, Buzzards, and Owls fly directly alongside me when I was walking home from school or traveling down the road in a car or truck. There were times during my shamanistic training in the wilderness when I woke up and found myself sleeping alongside a Black Bear, or being stalked for days by a Mountain Lion. I have slept with Rattlesnakes, had my hiking food stolen by a feisty Fisher, and fought with a Wolverine over my trout catch. A Wolf helped lead me out of the forest when I was lost, and Porpoises swam alongside me when I fell out of a boat. I even had a Great White Shark chase me out of the water at Moonstone Beach, California. One time in Nevada, a Gila Monster Lizard tried to attack me in a gas station bathroom. I have been encountering these spirits most of my life.

So as you can see, one way or another Nature is always communicating to me, and my life has never been boring; whether it be on the reservation, in the country, at work, while traveling, or in the city, one of Nature's creatures always went out of its way to get my attention. It couldn't simply be a coincidence. Symbolically, it had to mean something, whether the encounters and communication were strange or not. As I grew into adulthood, I could not help noticing that Nature communicates constantly, not only to me but to other people as well. I have seen my friends, relatives, colleagues, and even strangers also encounter unusual things from Nature. But they just brush the incident off, or they don't understand the message.

I have always tried to use such strange encounters as a learning experience. This has helped me develop skills in dealing with the phenomena. In time I've also realized that some signs, omens, messages, and encounters are culturally and geographically foreign to me. For example, one time my wife Tela and I were traveling through Florida and Louisiana heading back to California. We saw an Armadillo alongside the road at sunset. We knew it was a messenger, but we didn't know what it meant. At a later date I did some research on the Creek and Seminole Indians' mythology and learned what that animal meant to them in terms of a symbol, a meaning I did not understand at the time. So even now I still find myself being forced to study a new encounter, to analyze a new natural symbol, to discover new things in order to expand the depth and breadth of my knowledge of Nature's language. There are still many things I just don't know about, such as phenomena dealing with the Stars, or symbols related to Lightning and Thunder, Rainbows, the Moon, Sun, or animals out of my tribal-cultural territory. But I am curious, and willing to take the time to learn, because such knowledge and experiences serve to make my life more meaningful! I have learned from my elder mentors that a closer relationship to Nature does indeed bring meaning to our lives.

I believe we are all children of Nature. As a traditional Native healer, and like my mentors, I am not only concerned about individual healing cases and situations, but also about collective healing needs; healing of the individual in relation to the community, and healing of communities in relation to our environment. I am concerned about people gaining spiritual knowledge so that they can develop spiritually and heal their relationship with Earth and Nature. Otherwise we will continue to have a sick society. The Earth should not be treated as an enemy. We cannot simply assume that we have sole dominion over our planet. The Earth is a living and breathing organism that we depend upon for survival. When we get out of balance with Nature and the Earth we become sick, and a lot of people are sick today because they have allowed their society and communities to harm, hurt, molest, torment, desecrate, and exploit Nature without just cause, to treat Nature without proper reciprocity. Life proceeds in a circle; what goes around comes around! So much has already been lost because of civilization, technological progress, industrial development, and pollution. With this desecration has come a loss of knowledge, values, and spirituality. In the meantime, Nature cries out to us all for help. It is constantly communicating to all of us, but most people in modern society are not even aware of it, or they haven't learned how to interpret the communication.

Wouldn't it be nice if we all had similar connections with Nature? I believe we can, but we must first change the way we think about Nature and how we relate to the Earth. That is my reason for writing this book.

Nature's Symbols

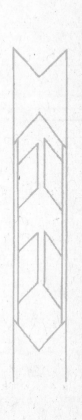

Our animal, bird, and other Nature relations are imbued with extraordinary life-giving powers and knowledge that can help us to survive and succeed in life. But in order to use this knowledge we must also learn the laws of Nature. For example, there is what I call the law of cosmic duality, which means that everything in our Universe and Nature has two sides to it: the physical and spiritual.

I also believe there is a law of reciprocity. We just can't keep taking from Nature without replenishing or giving something back in return. Otherwise we break the sacred circle and become responsible for creating our own problems with Nature.

Shamans have a primordial and special kinship with all things in Nature, and as a result they understand Nature's language and laws. They understand the symbolic communication from Nature, and they communicate Nature's meaning through their own system of symbols, for example, the regalia and artifacts that are still used in ancient Native rituals and ceremonies. These objects may include Eagle feathers, Bear claws and teeth necklaces, Deerskin hides, sacred pipes, Elkhide drums, rattles made from Deer hooves, Turtle shells, plant gourds, Wolfhide capes, Raven feather headdresses, medicine bundles, and ancient wooden masks, all symbols of Nature's communication. In fact, most indigenous artifacts and regalia are reflections and manifestations of the "natural objects and symbols" that come from Nature. And these power objects serve as a direct connection to Nature. Understanding the meaning and value of these symbols in mythology and ritual, and as they appear in our daily life, and using the symbols in a religious and spiritual way reminds us that we are an integral part of Nature. We are not separate from it, as the Western value system teaches us. This is why I believe that the ancient knowledge of our tribal shamans is so important to us all today.

What can we learn about natural phenomena from our Native elders and shamans? A symbol of power such as Hawk, might first appear in a dream, or series of dreams. Dreams can be vague, mysterious, and complicated, especially dreams that include symbols from Nature. When such an experience occurs, we are taught in our Native culture to seek counsel from an elder or shaman-mentor. When asking for help, we approach them with respect by offering pipe tobacco and a gift. In turn, they will teach us how to understand and learn to work with the messages. They help us to discover the meaning, purpose, and function of the symbols. Sometimes they teach us by telling us a story about a bird, animal, reptile, or fish; or by relating a parable or teaching an ancient myth.

Shortly afterward the dream symbol might manifest itself physically. For example, what would you think if you had a dream about a Woodpecker pounding on the front door of your house? And suppose you saw a real Woodpecker upon waking up in the morning or when going to work? Wouldn't you consider this out of the ordinary? What does it mean as a sign or omen? Now suppose you found some Wood-pecker feathers or a dead Woodpecker shortly after the dream and after encountering the omen? Would you think all of this was simply a coincidence, or would you want to talk to someone about the puzzle? If so, to whom?

In our Native American culture, when we can't understand what Nature is trying to tell us we believe we might lose the opportunity to connect with, acquire, and apply a new source of knowledge and power. Hence we seek out the advice of an elder or a medicine man/woman. We approach them politely and ask for their guidance. This doesn't necessarily mean that they are obligated to help us. But in most cases they will if we show them respect. Our elders are a store-house of rich knowledge, understanding, and traditional wisdom. They would tell me "Grandfather stories" about Nature, and they always had some kind of ancient myth to share. The elders and the shamans have a special way of perceiving the world, a humorous way of interpreting events, because to them Nature and everything that happens in it is a form of learning and entertainment. In Western society, however, most people don't have this opportunity, which is why I am trying to share such unique information and guidance here.

I gained much of my knowledge through this questioning process. I wasn't "psychic" twenty-four hours a day, seven days a week. I didn't understand everything that I dreamed about, nor did I under-stand every encounter I had with Nature. But I did have a cultural matrix and some basic understanding of the Native mythology, which in turn helped me to learn. I had all kinds of strange encounters while growing up, and these encounters took place in many different parts of the United States, wherever I went. It didn't make any difference whether I was in the wilderness, on farmland, near the ocean, in the country, or downtown in a large city. The messengers from Nature still come and visit me in the strangest places and at the strangest times. And I don't always understand what they are trying to tell me. Like me, you too will need to put some effort into studying the phenomenon. Don't expect an immediate answer to every question. If you can't find an elder to help you (and there were many times in my own life I couldn't speak with an elder), learn to work with the interpretations and exercises provided in this book and do your own research.

My knowledge also came from spending time in Nature. My learning experience was enhanced by undergoing shamanistic training and apprenticeships (I talk about this experience and background in my book *Native Healer*). The shamanistic training and the special time I set aside to spend in Nature served to further heighten my sensitivity, awareness, and understanding of natural symbols. My different mentors made me spend a lot of time observing and interacting with Nature. I was constantly gathering herbs, berries, and natural foods for the elders and my mentors. I was always outdoors cutting and chopping wood. I spent a lot of time fishing and hunting. Part of my shamanistic training required fasting, hiking, lamenting, and vision-seeking in Nature. I was taught to go out and study different birds in their territorial habitat. I had to remember what kind I saw, what color they were, how they behaved among themselves and with the other birds, and how they related to other creatures and their natural environment. In the meantime, different elders would tell me bird stories, about Raven, Eagle, Robin, Flickerbird, Hummingbird, Buzzard, Owl, Turkey, Grouse, Wren, and Finch. In this way I began to see some truth in the stories. I developed an understanding of the different birds and their different characters, their behavior, colors, personalities, and powers. The phenomena then became my teachers. For example, I learned why Blue Jay was considered a negative power, even though it is such a beautiful bird. It was always causing trouble by going around the forest spreading gossip and stealing other people's food. Its behavior and mannerisms were arrogant, selfish, and mischievous. I was told to talk to all birds, verbally and mentally, as a means of communication and to promote trust in the relationship.

The elders had me use the same approach in studying different animals, snakes, bugs, fish, frogs, and even plants and trees. I was taught not only to use my five senses in trying to identify and learn about my different "relations" in Nature, but I was also taught how to use my "sixth" sense in trying to communicate with them. I was taught to hold a Raven feather in my hand, to close my eyes and meditate while sitting in a very quiet, private, and isolated spot, and to use my mind, applying creative imagination, to see and hear the Raven, blocking out all other senses, focusing on one particular image. The feather, as a power object, was the symbolic key and connection. You might say I was taught to send out mental waves in order to communicate with the bird and try to get it to come and visit me. Sometimes it worked and sometimes it didn't.

This kind of learning takes a lot of concentration, practice, discipline, and commitment. I had to make personal time in my life to do it, between college classes, work, marriage, cultural events, obligations, and domestic duties. I didn't record my new encounters and experiences in a notebook, but stored them in my mind, or what some psychologists call the subconscious, where ancient archetypes and natural symbols are located. I meditated and used mental visualization exercises to help me learn how to explore the unconscious part of my mind-brain complex (which I will discuss further in the next chapter).

I was also taught by the elders how to use special creative techniques, such as visualization exercises performed in the sacred sweat lodge. Some modern people in Western society call this practice "imaging." I always made a ritual or ceremony out of my discipline. For example, I would light my pipe, offer it to the Great Creator, Nature, and to our "relations" on the Earth, and pray to them all. I smudged myself with cedar incense or sage as part of the invocation and meditative ritual. I talked to all good things in Nature this way and asked for their help. I asked them to help me see them, and to help me communicate with them mentally while in a dream, or while meditating in the sweat lodge. I used the sacred power of the cedar or sage to take off the negative human scent and negative human energy, and as a means of keeping away negative forces or interference. In the Native way, we always do this as part of the ritual and while praying, because according to our belief and understanding, the world is also full of bad spirits, ghosts, powers, and forces.

Sometimes this approach worked and sometimes my attempts at visualization were futile. Sometimes I could actually see myself sitting in a circle of birds and animals, talking to them in the human language, and in my mind, I could see and hear them talking to me. With years of practice, I was sometimes capable of performing the same feat in the physical world, by holding a meeting with the Ravens and Crows in a city park, for example.

I can remember occasions when I had dreams about flying with different birds, or running with different animals, and even turning into a bird or animal. This did not happen every time I tried to dream, to visualize, or to meditate with creative imagination. But it did happen sometimes, and to me it was real. It takes much commitment, discipline, and practice to learn how to develop this type of communication with Nature.

I also began to discover that some of the signs, omens, and interactions I had with different things in Nature didn't always mean the same thing to me as it did to my mentors. So I eventually developed a cultural-mental glossary of images that we all shared, but I also kept it flexible enough to fit my own perceptions, needs, and understanding.

These differences became clear to me during my training with a "Yurok Indian doctor," Calvin Rube. He was both highly respected and feared by the local Native people including the neighboring tribes. And he was the grandson of "Lucky from Wahsek," whom the famous anthropologist Alfred L. Kroeber recorded in his collective handbook and studies of the northwestern California tribes. I trained under Calvin as his apprentice for over ten years. He was a very difficult, strict, and dominating mentor. But he was also probably the most powerful and most effective Native healer I have ever met. He knew more about power training and application than any of the other elders I knew. He trained under Doc Benonie Harrie (Karuk), Doc Albert Thomas (Wintun-Pit River), Doc Charlie Klutchie (Wintun-Miwok), and, of course, his own mother and relations. His mother, Nancy Rube, whom some anthropologists documented in their classic works, was a highly respected Native doctor well known for her healing abilities throughout the Pacific and Northwestern Native communities. While working with Calvin I learned that he had a somewhat different understanding of the Hawk than the one my father had taught me. Such a difference can cause confusion, hence requiring more critical thinking, learning, and development of one's own system of knowledge in terms of dealing with the phenomena.

My father, Charles "Red Hawk" Thom, had taught me that the Hawk was a good sign, that it meant protection, and he was always happy to see it come in and fly around him. Calvin claimed he worked with the Hawk, too, but to him it had a dualistic message, or some-times conveyed even more meanings, all depending upon what kind of Hawk, how it was behaving, and what it was doing at the time. So he considered it a good bird but a bad sign. It warned him of danger, of enemies, of potential problems and conflicts, but could also be seen as a guardian and protector.

On one occasion, in late August 1980, I was staying at Calvin's house for spiritual training and as part of my shamanistic apprenticeship. He lived way back on the Yurok Indian reservation in California, high up on the side of a mountain, near Burrill's Peak, away from most other people. His house was very old, with no electricity or modern sewage system. And he considered himself "old-fashioned." He actually enjoyed using kerosene lamps, an old wood heater, and an outhouse. He raised chickens, pigs, and a few head of cattle, and had a small garden; but he mostly lived on traditional Native foods from the land which he gathered, fished, and hunted. He might have been poor by Western standards, but he owned a lot of ceremonial regalia and had a lot of traditional knowledge. He was therefore considered a "man of wealth" by local tribal leaders and the community.

One day I heard Eagles and Hawks screaming. I called for Calvin and he came outside the barn to look. We saw a strange sign: Several Eagles had gathered around the trees in the backyard of his farm, which in turn made the chickens start running around like crazy and squawking. Then a Red-tailed Hawk came in from the east, circled overhead, and began crying, as if challenging the Eagles to a fight. Four of them accepted and took flight. In a matter of moments they were circling, screaming, and diving at the Hawk, who managed to get above them and swoop down with claws outstretched, occasionally hitting a couple of them. Feathers started drifting down from the sky as the fight continued. The Hawk was faster and appeared to be winning the battle. At this point I saw Calvin bring out his pipe and pray. Then he sang a protection song. Shortly afterward a large Raven came in from the west, and it was hollering at the Hawk and Eagles. They then stopped fighting, and as the Raven came closer, each took off in a different direction. Calvin turned to me and said: "Thanks for letting me know. That was a bad sign. But things will work out OK now. You see how much power that Raven has? He didn't even have to fight. They all just ran from him because they knew."

I watched the entire scenario with intensity, trying to figure out what it all meant. Calvin had been reading my mind because he added: "The spirits are reporting into me. A group of ceremonial leaders will be coming up here sometime today to ask if they can borrow my regalia. I guess they are fighting and quarreling over their leadership and responsibilities, which can contaminate the regalia and hurt the people. So rather than getting involved in the possible conflict, I prayed for them in a good way. Now look over there, see Merk? [Yurok name for a rare Snowy Egret.] He is the 'peacemaker,' so everything will be just fine."

Later that day several different cars and trucks pulled up on the old farm, unannounced, carrying a number of different ceremonial leaders from different local tribes. Some of them started arguing as soon as they got out of their cars, and continued as they went into the house, nearly ending in a fistfight. But when they left with the regalia, they were all happy and supporting one another, and Calvin's prediction had come true. It is firsthand experiences like this that really help us to learn. In order to learn the secrets of Nature, to understand its symbolic language, and to reap its benefits we must also learn to use and practice a concept known as the law of reciprocity. As in the above-mentioned case, we make prayers to the Raven, appealing for help in the same way a person would go to a human family member or relative and verbally ask for help. We offer tobacco and/or food as payment; a gift in exchange for services that we hope will be rendered. Sometimes we make our prayers and pleas directly to the Great Creator, sometimes to Creation itself, and sometimes to the individual spirit of the Earth. In other situations, depending upon the need or problem, we go directly to certain powers that have a specific function upon this Earth.

For example, in northwestern California there is a sacred rock known as Rain Rock. It is located in the middle of the Shasta River, not too far from the small city of Yreka. The purpose of this rock is to

bring rain for the people during times of drought. There are many Indian stories about this sacred rock, but it takes a medicine man who has had specialized spiritual training and knowledge to recite an ancient myth, perform the proper ritual, and demonstrate the ability to use the power of the large rock to bring rain. How it all works is a mystery to science, but it does work! The Karuk Indian people know that the Great Creator placed the rock there to help human beings. So in this situation one is taught to go directly to the source of the power, the Rain Rock itself.

In other situations a person might go through a different kind of power that acts as a messenger between the Great Creator and man. For example, the Golden Eagle, the Raven, Frog, Turtle, Fish, or even a special kind of Snake can serve as a messenger between man and the Creator.

In addition, different tribes use different kinds of ancient myths and ceremonies to bring the natural powers to their aid, as in the case of the Hopi Indians in Arizona, who gather snakes, which in turn are used as messengers to the Thunder and Lightning spirits. By using mythic, natural symbols of the Earth in ceremony, they bring vital rain needed for corn crops and water needed for survival in this very harsh, hot desert environment. The average Westerner would have a difficult time understanding the actual meaning, purpose, and symbolic communication that takes place during this ceremony. He/she would consider it an act of magic, simply a coincidence, or would view the use of snakes for such purposes as repulsive. But it has worked for hundreds of years for the Native American people, who have learned how to develop and use a complex system of knowledge that is deeply spiritual in nature.

Almost all tribes across the continent have ceremonies that use song, ritual, dance, prayers, feathers, tobacco, regalia, and herbs as a means of communicating with the Great Creator, the forces of Nature, and the spirits. This is why they wear bird feathers in their hair, make prayer fetishes with bird feathers, use bird wing and tail fans, or even make complete outfits out of bird feathers. Each bird symbolically and spiritually represents a specific source of "power" and serves as a messenger, guardian, protector, or healer. Different birds symbolically communicate different messages. The Eagle, for example, is considered the biggest, strongest, and most courageous of all the birds. It can fly higher than any other bird. Hence it is capable of taking a message from the people on Earth to the Great Spirit via the sky. And other birds can be used as messengers to other powers and spirits in nature, in the water or on the Earth, across short distances or long. This is why you will even see some Native people dancing like a particular bird, making sounds imitating a certain bird or even using Eagle wing-bone whistles in ritual ceremony. The Sun Dancers blow the Eagle wing-bone whistle while dancing and praying, then shortly afterward it is common to see an Eagle come flying in from out of nowhere, directly over the Sun Dance.

When I need the Raven's help, I go outside and make a special prayer, hold the bird's feathers in my hand, and call out like a Raven. Usually when I do this a Raven or Crow will suddenly come in to find out what I want. It works for me, and it has worked for other people (you can read Catherine Feher-Elston's *RavenSong* for more examples).

I believe it works because it is an ancient system of communication that has always existed between humans and Nature, all of Creation and the Earth; whether someone else believes it or not is unimportant. Practice, experience, and social consensus, however, can help some people discover the truth and accept it as a reality. This is why Native myths and rituals are so important. The myth presents a certain theory, while the ritual provides people with an opportunity to test and experience the theory. Myth and ritual, when reenacted, serve to make the communication effective.

Perhaps believing in the knowledge helps make it all work, but I have seen Nature and the Earth communicate to people who were not raised in a similar belief system. The messenger physically appeared to them, but they did not understand it until it was brought to their attention and explained. Sometimes people seem to intuitively know that the sudden appearance of a bird, animal, bug, or snake is an omen. They "feel" or sense that such a phenomenon means something, but they don't know exactly what. Hence they just shrug it off in bewilderment or dismiss the incident as simply a coincidence.

Sometimes they would rather not recognize Nature's signs because then they don't have to consider their significance.

For example, a non-Indian friend of mine once told me that an Owl had been hooting at her house every night for the past several nights. At first she thought it was simply a coincidence, but when the Owl came back the second night, at exactly the same time, and sat in the same place, she began to develop an uncanny feeling. She said: "There was just something unusual about this large bird suddenly appearing out of nowhere, something about its behavior that bothered me. I felt disturbed and couldn't sleep. There was an uneasiness associated with it that I couldn't understand, so the third night it appeared, I knew it must mean something." I told my friend that the Owl was a messenger of sickness, evil, or death. If it comes around and hoots for a little while and leaves, then it is bringing you a message. If it continues to hang around, then it is a challenger. The message is symbolic, so one must study the message: What kind of Owl is it, what direction is it hooting from, how close is it, does it act aggressive or gloomy? To me, the message was plain. The next night my friend got a phone call; her brother had been involved in a car accident and was in the hospital in critical condition. With additional knowledge or spiritual assistance from a medicine man, the situation might have been averted or prevented from even happening. There are secret myths and rituals in our Native American heritage and culture that teach us not only how to understand the communication but how to use another form of communication and symbolic power as a means of overcoming fear and effectively dealing with the problem.

Thus, we have come to learn from Native stories, by way of instructions from our elders, and through personal experience that different animals have different powers, purposes, functions, and symbolic meanings. Among birds, for example, the White Swan represents the North direction, the first power of Creation, which is the Wind. The color white represents purity, strength, wisdom, and old age. The Red Flickerbird is considered a Fire bird. Its color is red, representing the East, which is the second power of Creation. It is the color and power of protection, rebirth, enlightenment, foresight, and illumination. The Yellowhammer or Meadowlark represents the third power of Creation, the Earth, from the South; its color is yellow. It represents the healing powers of the Earth, including the flowers and herbs, rocks, and all that is physical. It brings warmth, harmony, happiness, and security. The Raven's color is black; it is from the West, the last power of Creation, the Water. It represents the darkness, the unknown, the spirit world. It provides purification, protection, healing, and wealth.

Some of this esoteric knowledge is tribal-cultural specific, and some of it is common to all tribes. The four powers of Creation, the four directions, and the four elements might be represented by different colors and different kinds of birds and animals in different tribes. The ancient myths and Indian stories from different tribes teach us the meaning for a geographical area. One way to figure out the symbolic meaning and spiritual power of a bird, animal, snake, bug, and so on, in Nature is to study its appearance, character, behavior, and habitat. The Heron is a Water bird. The Hawk or Eagle is a Wind bird. The Turkey, Meadowlark, Quail, and Grouse are Earth birds. Such birds symbolically represent, and are connected to, the four powers of Creation: Air, Fire, Earth, and Water. Although the colors of these directions may vary somewhat among different tribes in our country, all tribal cultures recognize the symbolic importance of myths, ritual, and ceremony.

How to Develop Symbolic and Spiritual Thinking

The ancient myths and "Grandfather stories" teach us about the complex symbolism and interconnectedness of all things in Nature. The circle, for example, is one of the main symbols that can be used as a means of maintaining this interconnectedness. The shaman spends a lifetime studying and learning about this reality, including how to effectively deal with the symbols, or how to change certain symbolic realities. Some medicine men and medicine women, for example, can actually change the weather by using certain kinds of natural symbols. The symbols in this sense serve as "connectors" to certain powers; or they are, indeed, certain powers that need to be "activated." Prayer is the key that does the activating; the prayer might be verbal, through a song, by using a drum, a rattle, or a religious power object, via recitation of an ancient myth, by use of ritual in one's life, or through a telepathic communication from the mind.

Native Symbolic Thinking

The circle is an ancient, primal symbol, or what Carl Jung called a universal archetype. To the Native American, the symbol represents something that is sacred and holy. It represents unity, strength, protection, infinity, and spirituality. Thus, it is used in ritual, religion, art, architecture, ceremony, and social interaction. The following diagram depicts how Native myth and ritual function according to the cycles of Nature and life.

At each stage of one's life, as with the four seasons of Nature, myth, ritual, and ceremony are used as a means of helping a person adjust to a new spiritual transformation. This transformation is celebrated individually and collectively. It is right-brain-oriented, serves to develop intuitive skills, and in ancient times helped one achieve higher levels of accomplishment.

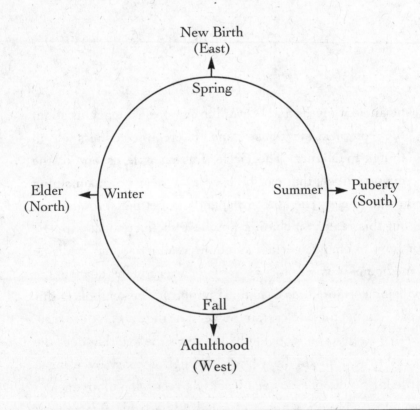

New Birth
(East)

Spring

Elder   Winter   Summer   Puberty
(North)   (South)

Fall

Adulthood
(West)

Symbolic Thinking Exercises

To help you increase your ability to use symbols, take a few minutes now and think about the symbolic power and meaning in names. Historically, some Native American people used names from Nature. Such chiefs and spiritual leaders as Handsome Lake, Cornplanter, Little Turtle, Black Snake, Red Cloud, Crazy Horse, Sitting Bull, Ten Bears, Dull Knife, Plenty Coups, and Lone Wolf derived their names from Nature; and their names had meaning and power. Other famous leaders had names from Nature, but in their tribal language, such as Tecumseh, Seatl, and Oceola. These names also had special symbolic meanings and served to connect them with certain powers in Nature.

In later years a lot of the Indian people lost their names because government agents and missionaries tried to convert Indian people to Christianity and Western civilization, for example Ely Parker, who was a famous Seneca chief and the first educated Native American to earn a college degree. In time some Native American people ended up with names such as Johnson, Smith, or Donahue, while others retained a combination of Western and Indian names, for example, John Fire Lame Deer.

Even today we can still find examples of Native people retaining family and tribal names from Nature or going back to Indian names, and among my acquaintances are Fools Crow, Mad Bear, Wilma Mankiller, Medicine Horse, Spotted Elk, Brown Eagle, Yellowtail, Martin Highbear, Old Elk, Buffalo-Horse, Old Yellow Hand, Red Hawk, Sunflower, and Badger. Some Native medicine men/women have secret names that serve as their passport to the Great Creator and the spirit world. They only use their special name while praying or during ceremonies, or when asking for spiritual help for the people.

Having a name from Nature is not just a fad or simply an Indian thing. The names have special meaning. Names serve to bond a person and family to Nature and are a constant reminder of one's kinship with the Earth. Some of the names are earned through a vision quest, some names are given in a cultural naming ceremony, and some of the names are inherited. In some tribes a person might have several different names until he/she becomes an adult and completes a spiritual initiation. All of my children have Indian names from Nature because I fasted for four days, sought visions, and was told by the ancestor spirits what to name each child. Their names give them special powers from Nature. In later years they will have to learn how to use these names in a spiritual way. In the meantime, I am trying to teach them the responsibility that goes with their names, the value of their names, and how the names can serve to empower them and give them cultural support, and can lead to a special relationship with Nature. Thus, in this way their lives will become more meaningful, and in turn, I hope, they will learn to have more respect and appreciation for Nature and spirituality in general.

What is your name? What does it mean? How does it connect you with Nature? What can be done to change your relationship with Nature and help make your own life more meaningful? Why not try to earn a secret name from Nature via meditation, vision-seeking, or through a prayer request and dream?

Perhaps this exercise and experience can help you: Go for a walk out in Nature. It could be a park in the city, on the outskirts of the city, or even in the country. You can also try this approach while camping, hiking, or backpacking somewhere near the ocean, in the forest, in the mountains, in the desert, or in other, more private places in Nature. Use such places as an experiment and a means of developing your learning. You might want to take a nature guide with you so that you can become familiar with the creatures in your geographical area. Then look for a quiet and personal place to pray, and perhaps perform this ceremony:

Put tobacco in your hand. Stand facing toward the east, offer it up to the Great Spirit and the four powers/directions of the Universe. First pray to the East, South, West, and then North. Did you notice that you symbolically and spiritually completed a circle, hence serving to bond you with the Mother Earth and the Great Circle of Creation? Make a short prayer something like this:

> Great Creator, the four sacred powers of the Universe, and all my relations in Nature, my name is———, I come before you in a humble manner and ask for spiritual guidance. I would like to learn how to communicate with and understand my relations in Nature, the animals, birds, bugs, plants, snakes, and other spirits. I ask that one of the relations who walk, crawl, fly, or swim come to visit me and teach me what your sign and message means. I would also like to have my own personal secret name from Nature.

Now sit down and be quiet, listen, observe, and learn. Watch everything around you. Study the behavior and characteristics of the creatures you see. Write down in a diary what you have observed. If you are not familiar with the birds or animals you encounter, then you need to look them up in a field guide. Did you see a Raven or a Crow, a Pigeon or a Flickerbird? What colors did it have? How did it behave? What was it doing? How close did it come? Try the same approach with other animals, bugs, snakes. See how close you can get them to approach you. Afterward be sure to thank them, and ask them to talk to you in a dream, in a language you can understand.

Try to figure out what this creature means to you in terms of a sign, omen, and/or power. Begin to develop your own spiritual coding system and a new basis for deciphering Nature's symbolic language. After some practice you should begin to distinguish the difference between a Muskrat and an Otter, a Robin and a Flickerbird, a Hawk and a Buzzard, a Garter Snake and a King Snake. Make up your own list of char-

acteristics that might help you understand what kind of power your relation in Nature has to offer. For example, you might categorize the animals you see according to the following characteristics:

- Cunning
- Fast, swift, aggressive
- Slow, careful
- Bold, courageous
- Demonstrates foresight, vision, clarity
- Strong
- Funny, playful

What creature was your favorite? Think why this animal was most appealing to you.

Try this technique as a means of learning more about how to relate to animals and Nature in a spiritual way. Start a new diary, and in it begin to develop your own modern myths about your experiences. For example, make up your own stories about what you saw and what you think the creature was doing, or what the creature was trying to say to you. Be sure to include a note about how all this affected your feelings and how it is beginning to change your perception of the world. How is this experience helping you to establish a kinship with Nature?

Share your experience with a friend or family members. Compare perspectives on what you saw, or what you think the creature was trying to communicate, and see what you can learn from your similar views or differences.

Refer to the chapters that follow on the signs and omens that I have come to learn and use. Spend time studying them. Try to memorize and internalize as much of the information as you can. In this way you will begin to develop what the psychologist Carl Jung called "ethnic archetypes/symbols" in your own unconscious mind. As stated before, some of the signs and omens might have different meanings for different people in different parts of the world, and for different people of different races and cultural backgrounds. Fundamentally, however, I think you will discover that there is some commonality. To continue your development, you should carry a diary and get in the habit of studying the signs you see in your daily life: Write down in your journal/diary what it was you saw (for example, a bug or a bird), what it is called, what color it is, how it was acting, and what it was doing or how it was behaving at the time. Write down what you think it was trying to tell you. In other words, as a sign and natural symbol from the Earth, what does the message mean to you? Compare your observations and experiences with those in the chapters on signs and omens; use these as a guide. Also, go to the local library and do research on the local bug, bird, and animal species, then compare this information with the beliefs, mythology, and culture of the local Indian tribe in your area. Study some of their myths, beliefs, and worldview. Now use this new knowledge to develop your own system of knowledge, and revise the list to fit your needs.

Mythic-Spiritual Thinking and Spirit Guides

Take a few moments here to pause from reading, to give your mind a break and to think about what has been shared so far. Refer to the following two charts. Study the box on page 44 relating to split-brain theory, with descriptions of the right and left hemispheres of the brain. Now compare it to the diagram I have provided of the conscious and unconscious parts of the mind.

Split-Brain Theory

Right Hemisphere	Left Hemisphere
Old Brain	New Brain
Theory and Abstract	Concrete and Sense-Oriented
Feminine	Masculine
Intuitive	Physical
Creative	Logical
Spiritual	Rational
Mythic-Symbolic	Written-Language-Oriented
Natural Symbols	Artificial Symbols

The old brain is considered primordial and therefore the basis of ancient archetypes, unconscious content, intuitive faculties, and mythic symbols. It is the home of creative imagination, dreaming, and symbols from Nature, and is oriented toward the spiritual and the feminine.

The new brain embodies the alternative mode of knowing. It is our conscious mind and therefore the basis for logical, linear, and rational thinking. It tries to dominate and suppress the unconscious content and knowledge. It is oriented toward the physical and the masculine, relying on the five senses for development.

A synthesis of both hemispheres of the brain leads to holistic learning and thinking, hence greater intelligence and a sharper intellect. Traditional Native hunters and shamans used both hemispheres of the brain in order to survive. Native mythology serves to develop both hemispheres.

As you can see, the concepts and symbols inherent in Native myths and Nature stories are located in and operate out of the subconscious part of the mind. This is the home of ancient and natural symbols, creative imagination, intuition, psychic powers, dreams, and visions. This is the space in our mind-brain complex where concepts, symbols, reality, and such phenomena as invisible playmates, spirits, talking animals or birds, the trickster, and hero archetypes all reside. The symbols can be positive or negative, masculine or feminine, physical or spiritual. And they all have a purpose, function, and meaning in terms of developing our intelligence, human potential, and spirituality.

Mind-Brain Complex
Jungian Theory as It Relates to Native American Thinking
by Medicine Grizzly Bear

Left Hemisphere	Right Hemisphere
Western-Society-Oriented	Primitive-Oriented
Physical-Oriented	Spiritual-Oriented
Masculine	Feminine
Logical	Intuitive
Rational	Imaginative
Linear-Digital	Cyclic-Holistic
Verbal-Language-Oriented	Mythic-Pictographic
Observation	Reflection
Abstract	Creative
Artificial Symbols (Man-made)	Natural Symbols

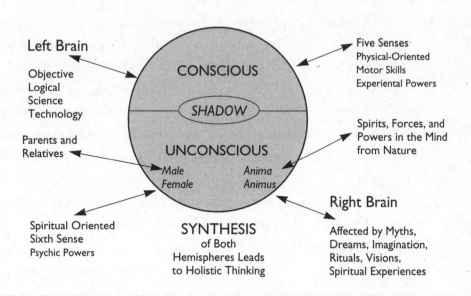

Left Brain
Objective
Logical
Science
Technology

Parents and
Relatives

Spiritual Oriented
Sixth Sense
Psychic Powers

CONSCIOUS

SHADOW

UNCONSCIOUS

Male
Female

Anima
Animus

SYNTHESIS
of Both
Hemispheres Leads
to Holistic Thinking

Five Senses
Physical-Oriented
Motor Skills
Experiental Powers

Spirits, Forces, and
Powers in the Mind
from Nature

Right Brain

Affected by Myths,
Dreams, Imagination,
Rituals, Visions,
Spiritual Experiences

Now, close your eyes for a moment. Think about an old story you were told when a child. Call it back from the deeper levels of your mind. (For example, something like Snow White, the Princess and the Frog, or an Indian story about Coyote.) Do you ever remember having an imaginary playmate? Do you think this imaginary playmate could have became your personal ally as a result of the stories you were told as a child? If so, how did this imaginary playmate empower you and serve as an ally when you were a child trying to solve life problems? Think about this seriously for a moment. Now, as an adult, could you still use an ally or spirit guide from Nature to help you? If so, of what value would such a resource prove to be in your personal life? Where could you find such a special, spiritual, and secret friend? Traditional Indian people and Native shamans have found their spirit guides in the ancient Nature stories.

The Native American system is one of constant bonding with the Earth matrix. There are specific myths that uniquely address the four essential stages of life, as Jung would call them, and these are interspersed with a variety of rituals and ceremonies. At each phase the Native member is given an opportunity to experience a new rite of passage, and this transformation has a profound effect upon the development of the left- and right-hemisphere dimensions of the midbrain. The appropriate myth-and-ritual combination therefore offers one an opportunity to synthesize the conscious and the unconscious, the logical and the intuitive, the masculine and the feminine, and the physical and the spiritual.

Symbols have power and meaning. Think about the circle for a moment. It has no beginning, it has no end; it is infinite. This is why we say it is sacred and holy. All of Creation is a great circle, our Universe is in a circle, life is in a circle, our sacred sweat lodges are in a circle, the medicine wheel is in a circle, most drums are shaped like a circle; the tepee and ceremonial lodges are in circles, and we even hold council in a circle because to hold a meeting in this way serves to dissolve potential conflicts and promote harmony. The symbol and power of the circle creates and promotes unity and wholeness.

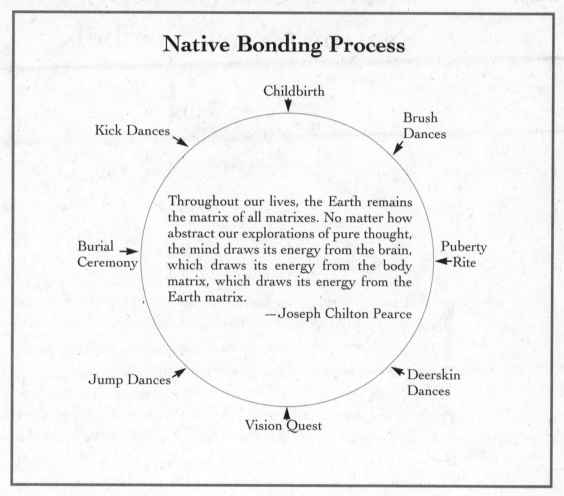

Native Bonding Process

Childbirth

Kick Dances

Brush Dances

Burial Ceremony

Throughout our lives, the Earth remains the matrix of all matrixes. No matter how abstract our explorations of pure thought, the mind draws its energy from the brain, which draws its energy from the body matrix, which draws its energy from the Earth matrix.

—Joseph Chilton Pearce

Puberty Rite

Jump Dances

Deerskin Dances

Vision Quest

Stories for Discovering Nature's Spirit Symbols

In our Indian heritage and culture we are taught that the myths are called "Grandfather stories." The intent of such stories was multi-faceted, often tribal and geographically specific, and usually appropriate for telling at certain times and for special reasons. Most Indian stories were told in the winter season of the year, however there were some exceptions to the rule. With most tribes an elder, shaman, or relative would tell a story of other times to help the children or a friend resolve a problem. A knowledge of the cultural symbolism was very important to understanding the story, whether the symbols were being described (spoken), drawn or carved (as on art and artifacts), and in all rituals, ceremonies, and healing. In most situations the symbols used to dramatize the myth or story reflected things in nature, such as the talking stick, prayer feathers, certain regalia, and power objects, while dramatizing a myth or story.

Knowledge was handed down from generation to generation

through oral communication, symbols, rituals, and artifacts. Some of these symbols can be found on cave drawings, or communicated through the Nature stories, songs, dances, ceremonies, and spiritual training. The ancient myths and stories were considered sacred teachings, hence treated with seriousness, reverence, and retention. The stories served a number of purposes, each designed for a specific task, situation, event, activity, or learning. Nature was the native people's laboratory and school. The concept of "power" was a significant part of the learning process. Myth served as a form of theory while ritual provided one with the opportunity to experience, synthesize, and internalize power. Our ancestors realized that the world was a Great Mystery, and could not be easily explained. It was complicated and very powerful. In order to survive, adapt, and succeed in life, one had to have power of one's own; a supernatural power such as one of the "relations" in Nature, an ancestral ghost, a special spirit guide, or a creation of one's imaginary guilt/aid. A considerable number of now recorded Native myths and Nature stories still address this need, reality, and purpose.

Considering that the Native myths are "ancient," modern students have the right to ask pertinent questions about the phenomena so far discussed, such as: "Of what value is this knowledge today, in the twenty-first century?" "Can the ancient teachings actually be used in modern life?" "Is the world still full of spirits, powers, potential dangers, and mystery, and do we need to relate to it in a supernatural way?" "Of what value are natural symbols and forms of communication in an artificial civilization?" Personally, I believe more than ever that we need a better understanding of Nature, and we need the ancient tools and knowledge in order to adapt to the constant change and challenges that both the natural world and the newly created artificial world present to us.

Here are a few modern examples and experiences of my own to

demonstrate this point. One day I was traveling with a colleague from Gonzaga University in Spokane, Washington, to Lopwai, Idaho. We were scheduled to conduct an Indian education training workshop on the Nez Perce reservation. We were approximately thirty miles down the road when all of a sudden a Hawk flew in from the right. I told my Colville Indian friend: "Hey, Glen, you better be careful. There is danger up ahead on the right!"

I encouraged him to slow the car down and be observant. In a few minutes a Cow started to cross the road from the right. It just mysteriously appeared from out of the high grass. There was no possible way we could have seen it from a distance. Luckily, we were going slowly and my friend was driving defensively, and he managed to avoid hitting the large animal. The car behind us, however, was not so lucky.

My friend was scared and shook up. He turned to me and said: "How did you know, are you psychic or something?" "No," I replied, "I simply first felt the Hawk, then I saw it. It is an example of Nature's language trying to communicate with us." Then I continued, "It is a good bird and a good power, but a bad sign; it means danger."

So to the traditional Indian, nothing is a coincidence, everything happens for a reason, and the world is indeed a dangerous, mysterious, and challenging place. After that, my colleague began to tell me all kinds of old Indian stories he had heard as a child from his tribal elders and medicine people about different birds, animals, snakes, and powers in Nature, both good and bad. By the time we got to the reservation we saw a flock of Ravens eating something on the road. I turned and asked my colleague: "What does that mean?" He studied it for a few minutes and said: "It is a good sign. I guess it means a lot of people will show up for the meeting, there won't be any conflict, and they will probably have a potluck for us." His prediction, or should I say natural foresight, was accurate.

In the Indian way, our elders don't explain everything in detail to us. Indian myths and Nature stories have traditionally been taught to the young, family members, and visitors in a variety of different ways, depending upon the tribal background. In some tribes the Elders taught the stories in the winter season, or upon need. In some tribes the stories were shared mainly by a "storyteller," a special person who had been trained since childhood to learn, memorize, and transmit the ancient knowledge, symbolism, and ideology to other members of the tribe. In other tribes the shamans did the storytelling during certain rituals, rites, ceremonies, and sacred dances. Others used a combination of different approaches. One way or the other, the people always made a concerted effort to pass the oral tradition down from one generation to the next—at least until forced assimilation and Western education impacted our cultures. They want us to use our imagination and figure it out for ourselves. One story might have several different meanings for different people, but in other situations it might have a common meaning. Thus, both hemispheres of the mind-brain complex are needed in order to learn, think about, and apply the ancient and natural knowledge.

Realizing that most Western, non-Indian people have not been taught and trained in this different cultural context, I will try to provide a guide that you can use while reading the following stories. They are a short collection of some of my favorite myths and Nature stories, which I have learned from Native elders and medicine people from different parts of the country. I would like to share it here to provide a good cross section of material to illustrate the points I have tried to explain above. Use the following rhetorical questions as a guide to help you understand the symbols, meaning, philosophy, and knowledge contained in each story.

- What is the message and purpose of this myth/story?
- What are the natural symbols being used in the myth/story?

- What do the symbols mean, and how can you learn from them?

Here are a few of my favorite stories. As a learning exercise, I want you to read and study the stories several times. (You may want to make a tape recording of the stories and listen to some of them at night just before you go to sleep.) With the use of a diary begin to describe your personal imaginary playmate, if you had one. If you did not have one as a child, then make one up now—a personal spirit guardian from one of the Indian stories. Write a short paragraph about what story symbols mean to you. You can even talk about how these symbols make you feel: sad, happy, weak or strong, afraid or bold, sexy, insecure, aggressive, adventurous, passive, protective, healthy, unhealthy, intelligent, ignorant, spiritual, psychic, whatever.

The Woman Who Feared Snakes (Wiyot)

Many, many winters ago, there was a woman who was deathly afraid of snakes. Because she was young, people were curious why she always carried a cane. She would tell them: "I hate snakes. If I see any, I will beat them with my special stick."

One day she started out early in the morning to do her chores. She went to the marsh to gather roots, reeds, and herbs. She packed them all in her Indian-made burden basket. Deciding it was full, she bent over to lift it up and strap it on her back for easy carrying.

As she tried to pick up the basket she noticed it was stuck on something, or perhaps a little too heavy. So she pulled harder, but it still didn't budge from the ground. Puzzled, she began to look around for the problem and noticed that a big Snake was holding it.

Then the Snake spoke to her. It said: "You're afraid of me. So I'm going to make you go with me. Just leave that pack basket there." He must have used his power on her, because she left with the big Snake. Finally they got to the river, then he turned and said: "Climb into my mouth. Once inside, you will be safe. Don't fear if I have to swallow you all up. I am going to take you to my lodge." And that is what she did.

The Snake dove into the middle of the river and carried the woman all the way down to the bottom where he lived, directly into his house. It even had a fire inside of it, because he was using water-soaked spruce, the kind that burns like pitch. Even when it is wet it burns well.

He made a wife of the Indian woman, and they had babies. The baby Snakes grew and began to ask questions about their mother, why she looked so different. They decided they wanted to meet their human relations and grandparents. So she told them one day, "Go south, and look for humans. The one with the three markings on her chin, that is your grandmother."

So the young snakes made their journey and found the house of their grandmother. The old lady had a big cane and started to beat them. She didn't like snakes. She said she would kill them all, and so they got scared and left. The young Snakes went home and told their mother. The mother cried and told them: "I will go and tell her you are her grandchildren. Now get in my pack basket." So she took them all back to explain to her mother; but still the old lady didn't like snakes. She chased them all away.

And that is why some snakes come to visit us, some can be nice, some are challengers and bad signs. Either way, however, the elders teach that snakes are never supposed to be in the house, even if they come as a friend or relative to visit, to give us a message or power. To have a Snake in the house is a bad sign and bad luck.

Grizzly Bear and Raven (Lummi)

▼▼▼▼▼▼▼▼▼▼▼▼▼▼▼▼▼▼▼▼▼

A long time ago, in the Beginning, Raven was helping the Great Spirit create the world. He had the power to change streams, replace trees, and spread things around so all the same trees didn't grow in one place. Raven even guided the birds and animals to different places so they wouldn't be crowded.

Grizzly Bear was also busy working, gathering his herbs and getting healing instructions from the spirits, and between sessions taking time to eat berries. He loved berries.

One day Raven got hungry and tired and flew down by the river to rest. He was walking around looking for something interesting to eat when all of a sudden he heard big tree limbs breaking, rocks coming down the side of the bank, and a loud growling noise. It startled Raven, so he hollered: "Hey, who is making all that noise?"

Well, you just don't talk to a Grizzly Bear like that. So Grizzly Bear got mad. He stood up, sniffed, and looked around with his huge arms and claws outstretched, ready for a challenge. He roared out a warning: "Who is it that thinks they have so much power to challenge me?"

Raven got scared, but he is a fast thinker. He responded, "Oh, cousin, is that you over there, Grizzly Bear? I made a special trip, just to come and see you, so I hollered to get your attention. And I have a special message for you from the Great Spirit."

Well, Grizzly Bear humbled himself when he heard that. And in accordance with custom and law, he invited Raven to come to his home and eat with him. Grizzly Bear hollered across the river: "Hey, cousin, I am happy that you came to visit. You must be hungry from all the hard work you have been doing around the world. Follow me to my lodge, where we can eat, rest, visit, and pray with each other."

Raven went to Grizzly Bear's lodge. Inside the cave was a warm fire, and hanging from the wall were strips of smoked salmon, deer meat, berries, and lots of roots and other foods. Grizzly Bear told Raven: "Here, cousin, sit down and pull your stool close to the fire to warm yourself. Let us visit for a while, and then I will fix something to eat."

While Raven was looking around the room, his stomach growled from smelling and seeing all that good food. In the meantime, Grizzly Bear reached over and got a shell, placed it under his feet, which he then propped up by the fire. He was making medicine this way, and as the fire got hotter it caused grease to drip from his feet into the shell.

So Raven talked and talked while trying to wait patiently and respectfully. Grizzly Bear kept checking the shell to see if it had filled up yet, and noticed that Raven was becoming impatient. So he turned and said: "Hey, cousin, I heard you have a beautiful doctor song. My back and feet have been hurting a lot lately, so I'll offer you this tobacco and these gifts if you will sing that song for me."

(I bet you didn't know that a long time ago, Ravens could actually sing instead of just squawking!)

So Raven sang, "Hey-yo, hin-no-way-yo, hey-yo-hin-no-way-yo," four times. Four times he brushed his large wing feathers over the Grizzly Bear's back, pulled a dark shadow off, and threw it in the fire.

Bam! It spattered, popped, and burned causing both of them to jump up in fright.

Grizzly Bear noticed that he was feeling much better. He wasn't stiff and sore anymore. So he offered food to Raven, encouraging him to dip the dry meat into the shell full of grease.

Raven thought that was the best food he'd ever eaten. The next morning upon leaving he said: "Hey, cousin, what is your secret in cooking?" But the Grizzly Bear just laughed and waved good-bye.

About a year passed and these two met up again. This time it was the Grizzly Bear who was wandering around in the Raven's territory by the ocean coast. Once again the Raven heard a bunch of noise and someone growling around, so he called out, and soon discovered it was Grizzly Bear. All year he had thought about the secret in the food; if only he could have a chance to show his magic and medicine in return, as a form of respect and reciprocity. So he hollered: "Hey, cousin, is that you, Grizzly Bear?" And the huge bear stood up with a handful of medicinal roots. "Yes, it is, my cousin, what are you doing?" The Raven then invited Grizzly Bear to his home, hoping now he could prove his power.

So he pulled a large log up next to the fire and asked Grizzly Bear to sit down and warm his feet. In the meantime, he secretly hid an abalone shell under his claws while letting the fire get hotter and hotter. He asked Grizzly Bear to sing for him while he waited for his claws to melt. As Grizzly Bear got up and sang and danced around, Raven put his feet closer to the fire. Then Grizzly Bear said: "Hey, cousin, you are a good singer. Get up and sing and dance with me." "No," replied Raven, "I don't want to show you up." He was trying to buy time to get his claws to melt grease into the shell, along with herbs, so he could make medicine like Grizzly Bear had done.

All of a sudden his feet got too close to the fire and caught on fire. He jumped up and started squawking, jumping up and down as if crazy, until finally he jumped into the creek. Grizzly Bear was embarrassed and left; he felt outdone and humiliated. And that is why to this day the Raven's feet are all crooked and black all over, and that is why the Raven is no longer a good singer. He is a powerful doctor, but not a good singer. But still you will sometimes find the Raven and Grizzly Bear together, making medicine to help others, or sometimes just fooling around together in Nature, trying to outdance each other along the river or creek.

Coyote and Wolverine (Cheyenne)

One time Coyote's wife had a secret lover named Wolverine, but Coyote didn't know about it. He and his wife were out hunting one day, and when they came upon Wolverine's lodge they decided to visit. They asked permission to go inside. Wolverine got all nervous and was surprised to see Coyote.

"Come in," he said anyway, and, trying to act friendly, asked, "What are you hunting?" In the meantime, he was trying to check out Coyote's weapons and power. He prodded further, curious to know if Coyote knew that he was sneaking around with his wife. "Why have you come to my lodge?" he kept asking nervously. Finally, Coyote got annoyed and replied: "Oh, I think I will hunt Wolverines."

He didn't really mean it, he just said it hoping to shut Wolverine up. He really wanted a place to rest and sleep. But this frightened Wolverine, who then ran immediately out of the tepee. Being curious, Coyote followed. Then Coyote's wife followed because she too was getting nervous.

Seeing that he was being followed, Wolverine thought fast. "Hey, Coyote," he said, laughing, "I bet my canoe is longer and better than yours."

Coyote didn't like being talked down to, so he went over and got his canoe, then put it alongside Wolverine's. While he was measuring the size, Wolverine grabbed Coyote's wife and pulled her into his canoe, then started paddling off downriver. Coyote got mad and jumped into his canoe, thinking it was all just a game, and took off after them.

As he got closer, a strange thing happened. He heard Wolverine singing a song; then suddenly the fog came and completely surrounded him; he couldn't see anything. He realized that this was how Wolverine made his medicine, but it was too late and he got lost.

For days he stayed at home thinking. He was very sad and lonesome for his wife. He even went down to his canoe, looking out over the water, and cried. He even tried talking to his paddle. He asked the paddle where his wife was and what he could do to get her back. Finally, the paddle talked to him and said, "Some things we have to figure out on our own."

Well, this made Coyote very mad, so he urinated and defecated all over the place, cursed the paddle, and broke it up. He made so much noise that his two friends came out of the woods to see what was going on. It was Marten and Fisher.

They told Coyote they could help, and they did. When they got to Wolverine's house they walked all over his ceiling, walls, and roof. It was as if they had special magic, then the fight between them began. Other people came to watch and they wanted to know how Marten and Fisher had this special kind of power. How could two people like this be so quiet, sneak up on their enemies, and even walk upside down so fast all over the place, and yet remain unharmed?

Coyote got so mad about the two friends showing off that he killed everyone. He went and found his wife and headed home, constantly growling at her and threatening her, but he eventually gave her another chance. In the meantime, all the Indians who had been watching at a distance also followed Coyote home. They wanted to know the secret of these different animal powers, and they pleaded with Coyote to teach them. They promised to always leave him food when hunting, and they promised to never be his enemy or to hurt him or his family. Thus, Coyote consented and taught them the secret warrior medicine of Wolverine, Fisher, and Marten, but not everything about his medicine. The elders say that a man who has Coyote's medicine can never be killed.

Creation of the Animal People (Shasta-Karuk)

A long time ago, the Earth was once a human being. The Great Creator made her a woman. The soil is her flesh, the rocks are her bones, the wind is her breath, the trees and grass and the rivers and streams are her veins. She lives spread out, as if lying down in a nurturing position, so that we can all live upon her. If we should do her any wrong, she will let us know by moving, and it will come in the form of earthquakes and floods. If she gets mad or sick, she will let us know by the fire and heat that will come out of the volcanoes.

After changing her to Earth, the Great Creator took some of her flesh and rolled it around into small balls, just like you see some people do with mud. It was from the first mud balls that humans were created, and they were considered the "First Human Beings." In physical form, some were half human and half animal, half bird and half human, or half human and part fish, and so on. That is why some of them could fly like birds, run like animals, or swim like fish. And they all had special powers and could communicate via telepathy, which is the original language. Because of their special powers they were more powerful and cunning than either animals or humans, but in some ways they were considered stupid. For example, they knew they had to hunt in order to survive. But they did not know which animals were actually people and which were really animals, so sometimes they ate humans. But even back in those days there were also human-type people like we have today. They were the Indians, or ancestors, but some say they were not as smart as we are today.

Because the original Indians were strong but not too smart, the other creatures in Nature felt sorry for them. Some of the animals, birds, reptiles, and fish shared their knowledge and power with the humans. In those days they even sang and danced with each other to celebrate good fortune, or to give thanks to the Great Creator, and to pray and give thanks to the Earth. We were told that we should respect everything, and if we took good care of the special gifts and powers, we would survive. But we were also warned that if we abused the gifts and powers, we would be punished. And so it has been from the very Beginning. Some of the original creatures have disappeared, but their spirit side is still around in places on the Earth. That is why one has to be careful about what they do to the Earth at all times. We should learn to respect and care for it; otherwise the spirits of Nature and the Earth itself will turn against us.

Coyote and Skunk (Crow Nation)

There was a place where a lot of Prairie Dogs and Rabbits were living. Coyote used to travel there a lot, but he didn't know how to catch them. He sat down by the stream and thought, "Maybe I could change the course of this stream and drown them all?"

After a while Skunk came by and asked, "What are you thinking about?" Coyote told Skunk his idea, and then the two of them devised a plan. Skunk went upstream and got some slime grass. Then Coyote laid on some driftwood while Skunk stuffed the slime grass, which looked like a bunch of maggots, in Coyote's ears, eyes, armpits, mouth, and all around him. After this was done and Coyote looked dead, Skunk went and told the Prairie Dogs and Rabbits that Coyote was dead, and if they didn't believe it, they should come and see for themselves.

It was getting to be a very hot day, so while Coyote waited he wished for a cloud. Shortly afterward one appeared. Then he wished it would sprinkle just a little bit to help cool him off. Then it began to sprinkle rain. But it was still hot, so Coyote wished it would rain so hard that the storm would cause the water to come up around his legs, and it did. After a while the storm got so bad, and the water got so high, that Coyote was washed downstream on the driftwood, and landed in a wood jam.

Sometime later Skunk came by and was looking for Coyote. When he found him he put more grass in his ears, mouth, armpits, and around his tail. Then he went over and told the Rabbits and the Prairie Dogs that the person they feared so much was dead.

At first two Rabbits came over to see if Skunk was telling the truth—Jack Rabbit and White Rabbit. They still didn't believe Skunk, so he got a stick and hit Coyote in the stomach with it. They went back and told the others that Coyote was indeed dead. But the others did not believe it, so more of them came to inspect the body. But they still didn't believe it, so Skunk got a bigger stick and hit Coyote harder. Finally the Prairie Dogs were persuaded to come, and they looked at all the maggots in Coyote's mouth, ears, armpits, and all over. So now everyone believed Coyote was dead.

More of the animals got curious, and a little braver, and they all gathered around Coyote. Skunk told them they must have a special dance because their enemy was dead. The Rabbits and Prairie Dogs all danced around Coyote in a circle. They were having a great time. All of a sudden Skunk said, "Hey, look up there in the sky, is that a

Hawk or something?" While they were looking Skunk sprayed them all in the eyes with his stink liquid and smell. Once they couldn't see or smell, Coyote grabbed the sticks that Skunk had hit him with and he started to club the animals one by one. Only a few of them managed to get away.

Coyote built a fire and told Skunk to carry the Rabbits and Prairie Dogs over. So Skunk brought over four big loads. Then he cleaned all the animals and singed their hair. He was doing all the work while Coyote supervised. Then Coyote told Skunk to put the animals in the fire pit with some saltbush. He buried them with only the tails sticking up.

While the meat was slowly cooking, Coyote instructed Skunk to rest in the shade with him. They waited and waited for the food to cook. Coyote then said: "Hey, cousin, I am bored, what about you? Why don't we have a race to the mountains? Whoever wins can eat all the Prairie Dogs and Rabbits."

Skunk protested: "No, I can't run fast at all. Anyway, all the way to the mountains is too far for a run." But Coyote kept pestering the Skunk until he finally consented, with one condition. "Since I am a slow runner, let me have a head start, over there by the first hill." Although Coyote was a little leery, he agreed, and Skunk took off.

When Skunk reached the first hill he looked around for a Badger hole. He found one and pulled a tumbleweed in behind him. Soon Coyote ran past like a whirlwind. Skunk came out of the hole and went back to where the food was cooking. The Rabbits and Prairie Dogs were just right, very tender and juicy. So he took the meat out of the pit, cut off the tails, and put them back in the pit, trying to make it look undisturbed. Then he went up on a high rock and started eating.

Just as Skunk was finishing his meal, Coyote came back all tired. He was sweating and out of breath. He looked around but didn't see Skunk, so he walked over to the stream and bathed in order to cool off. Then he went over to the fire pit to check on the food. Once again he looked around and said: "Well, Skunk has such short legs he will take forever to get here. I'm hungry, and besides, I won anyway."

He reached down and pulled on the animal tails. "Gee," he said, "this food must really be tender because their tails came right off!" This only made him hungrier, and he looked around for a stick to dig them up with. He kept digging and digging all over, but still he couldn't find any Prairie Dogs or Rabbits. He got so mad that he hollered all over: "Skunk did this to me! When I find him I am going to kill him!" Ever since that time you never see Coyote and Skunk together. They are enemies, and that is why Skunk always runs whenever he smells or sees Coyote coming around.

Coyote and Eagle
Visit the Land of the Dead (Yakima)

Way back in the Beginning of Creation, our people considered the animals to be people also. We did a lot of things together, including participating in sacred dances, ceremonies, and healing. We helped each other in many ways and learned from each other. Coyote was especially fond of humans. He became very sad one day because all the humans around him were dying. They left and went to the land of the spirits. Now Coyote, who likes to think a lot, heard so much crying going on that he thought about how he could bring the dead back to the land of the living.

As the situation got worse, Coyote's sister died. Then some of his friends died, too. Even Coyote's best friend, Eagle, lost his wife and was mourning over her. To comfort him, Coyote came up with a plan. "The dead shall not remain forever in the land of the deceased," he said boldly. "They are like the leaves that drop from the trees, brown and dead in the fall time; but they shall come back to life just like in the springtime, when the birds use their power to sing and bring back new life."

But Eagle did not think he could wait that long. He wished the dead could be brought back without any further delay. So Coyote and Eagle decided to start out together on the path that leads to the land of the deceased. Eagle flew while Coyote trotted, both looking brave and also scared. After several days they came to a big body of water. It was a spooky place. On the other side they could see a lot of lodges.

"Let's get a boat," hollered Coyote. "And we'll go across the water."

Coyote shouted and shouted, but nobody would answer. He squinted to look closer but could see no movement on the other side. Eagle tried looking with his sharp vision and said, "We came all this way for nothing. There is nobody on the other side."

"No," said Coyote, "they are all just sleeping." He looked around again and continued talking: "Don't you know that the dead people sleep during the day and come out only at night? So we'll just wait here until dark."

After sunset Coyote began to sing his power song. In a short while four spirit men came out of the houses, got into a boat, and came across the big body of water toward Coyote and Eagle. Coyote continued to sing while Eagle prayed, and the spirit men kept rhythm to the song with their paddles. It was like magic, as if the boat was just floating on top of the water by itself.

Soon the boat arrived and Coyote and Eagle got in with the ghosts. They could heard drums playing and singing and dancing as they got closer to the old village on the other side. Just as they were about to step out of the boat, a spirit man warned: "Don't go into the houses. Do not look at things around you. Just keep your eyes closed because this is a very sacred place."

Coyote challenged the ghost. "But we are hungry and cold," he said. "We have come a long way to get here, and according to custom should be fed."

So they were allowed to go into a large lodge made of tule mats, where the spirits were dancing and singing to the beat of the drum. An old woman soon approached them with some food and a basket full of oil. Using a feather, she dipped it into the oil and fed them until their hunger was gone.

The Eagle looked around. Inside the large lodge he saw that everything was beautiful, and there were many, many spirits. They were dressed in the best ceremonial regalia, beautifully decorated with shells and Elk's teeth. Their faces were painted and they wore feathers in their hair. The Moon, hanging above, filled the big lodge with a special spiritual light. Near it stood Frog, who has watched over the Moon ever since it jumped into it a long time ago. He made sure that the Moon gave light to everyone. The entire scene was very mystical.

Coyote had another plan. He waited until the dancing and singing hit its peak, then he reached over and snatched the Moon from Frog. He swallowed it. In this way he created darkness. Then Eagle caught the ghosts one by one and put them in a large basket. He closed the lid tight so they could not escape. Then both Coyote and Eagle ran with the basket back toward the boat, on the water's edge.

Along the way they heard noises in the basket and stopped to listen. "The people are coming back to life," said Coyote. "See, it is working."

Then they heard someone say: "Why don't you let us out?" But Coyote and Eagle were somewhat afraid of what would happen. After a while they had to walk because the basket got heavier. Coyote finally decided to let them all out, as more spirits turned into people and the basket became too heavy to carry.

But Eagle protested. "No," he hollered, "don't do that!" But it was too late, Coyote had already dropped the basket. Much to their surprise, when all the spirits came out they were still in ghost form, and moving like the wind, they went back to the land of the dead.

Eagle was very upset and he screamed at Coyote for a long time. As they sat down to think about the situation, Eagle remembered what Coyote had said. "It is not yet autumn, the leaves are still falling, just as people die, so why don't we wait until spring?" he said to Coyote.

"No," Coyote growled back, "I am tired of all this. Let the dead stay in the land of the deceased forever." So Coyote made the law that after people have died they shall never come back to life again. If he had not opened the basket and let the spirits out, the dead would have come to life every spring when the new leaves come to life and the flowers begin to bloom; and that is also why today the living humans and the dead are not supposed to be together.

Coyote Takes Water from the Frogs (Wintun)

One time Coyote was out hunting and he found a dead Deer. While trying to decide what to do, he suddenly noticed that one of the Deer's ribs looked just like a big dentalium shell, which is highly prized as Indian money, and he picked it up. He went up to see the Frog people. The Frog people were guardians of all the water. The Creator put them in charge so that other people wouldn't take the value of water for granted. When anyone wanted any water to drink or cook with, or to wash with, then they had to go and get it from the Frogs.

Coyote came up to them and said: "Hey, you Frog people, I have a big dentalium shell to offer as payment for a big drink of water. And I would like to drink for a long time because I am really thirsty from all that hunting."

The Frogs held council and the leader said: "Give us the shell and you can drink all you want."

So Coyote gave them the shell and began drinking. The water was behind a large Beaver dam, and this is where Coyote drank and drank. Looking around in a sneaky manner, he lifted his head and hollered: "Hey, Frog people, I am really thirsty. Don't worry about me if you see my head down for a long time, OK?"

"Sure, it's fine with us," they hollered back. Coyote drank for a very long time. Finally, the leader got concerned and said: "Hey, Coyote, don't you think you have had enough? What are you doing over there?" The Frogs all hollered together, but Coyote kept on drinking.

The Frog people then started getting angry with Coyote and threatened him: "You sure are drinking more than your fair share of water. Perhaps you better give us another dentalium shell!" They wondered how a person could drink so much water, and figured he must be up to no good.

In the meantime, Coyote lifted his head and said: "Well, just let me have one more drink and I'll quit. I want the colder water on the bottom." All the time he was digging out under the dam. That is why he had his head down so far under the water. When he finished he

stood up and hollered: "Wow, that was great water, just what I needed."

Then, as he was about to leave, he faked a slip and fell back on the dam, causing it to break, and all the water went rushing down into the valley. It made a lot of beautiful waterfalls, rivers, streams, creeks, and even some lakes and ponds.

The Frog people were just as angry as can be, but they were afraid of Coyote. They hollered at him once more: "Darn you, Coyote, you took all our water." But Coyote just laughed and replied, "It is not right for only one group of people to have all the water. Now it is in places where everyone can have it, and I am sure they will still respect it." Coyote did that, and that is why we call him a trickster.

The Toughest Snake of All (Kickapoo)

A long, long time ago, all the Snake people got together for an annual powwow and social gathering. This was a good time for one to choose a mate. Snakes came from all over, of many different colors, striped and spotted, short and long, with fangs and toothless, slow and fast. As the women began to look around and select a mate, an argument developed as to which snake was the best-looking, who had the most power, who could run the fastest, and who was the toughest all around. So it was decided to hold a racing contest.

They all lined up: Black Snake, King Snake, Bull Snake, Gopher Snake, Copperhead, Rattlesnake, Garter Snake, even the Cotton-mouths and Water Snakes. Black Snake, often called the Blue Racer, proved to be the fastest, but Rattlesnake got mad and tried to fight him. He was so mad he wanted to kill him. Then they all got into the act. There was a terrible ruckus, which caused a rain- and hailstorm.

When the wrestling match was all over, King Snake proved to be the strongest, fastest, toughest, and best snake of them all. Even to this day he is considered the favorite among the Indian people.

How the Deer Got His Horns (Cherokee)
▼▼▼▼▼▼▼▼▼▼▼▼▼▼▼▼▼▼▼▼▼▼▼▼▼▼▼▼▼▼

When the world was first created, Deer did not have any horns. His head was smooth, just like a doe. But he was a great runner and could protect himself that way. The Rabbit was also a great runner and jumper, and they often played together. The other animals wondered who was the fastest and who could actually run the longest. They had a council meeting and decided to hold a contest between Deer and Rabbit. Beaver made a nice pair of antlers from the wood, and it was decided to use this as the prize for the winner.

The day for the contest was decided, and the rules were laid down. The runners were to start together from one side of a thicket and go through it, then turn and come back. The one who came out first was to get the horns. The antlers were put down on the ground at the edge of the thicket to mark the starting point.

Rabbit said: "Wow, I could really use those horns to protect myself." Then he looked around and cried out: "I don't really think this is fair. I don't know this part of the country, so I want to take a look around in the bushes first." The rest of the animals thought that was OK, and they let the Rabbit go into the thicket. After a while he was gone so long they became worried. They figured he was up to some kind of trick, so they sent a scout out to search for him. The Rabbit was caught gnawing at the bushes and pulling them away until he had made a secret road, a trail that would be easier for him to run through.

The Rabbit continued to work, not realizing he was being watched, and then the scout came back and reported to the council that the Rabbit was making a secret path all the way through the thicket to the other side. They didn't like what they heard. Finally, the Rabbit came out and said he was ready to start. The other animals accused him of cheating, but the Rabbit pleaded that he'd just gotten lost. The other animals agreed that such a trickster should not enter the race at all, and they awarded the antlers to Deer. That is why today we say that Rabbit is Deer's little brother. Whenever you see a Rabbit you can bet that a deer is someplace close by, but sometimes Deer runs so fast you can hardly see him in the thicket.

The Sister's Wish to Marry a Star (Chippewa, Cheyenne, Lakota)

A long time ago, according to our legends, there were two girls who were talking foolishly. This was back in the days when all the animals and birds, and our different relations in Nature, could talk together with understanding. These two girls decided to sleep outside, under the stars and open sky, instead of inside the lodge.

Well, you know how young people can be, full of fantasy and

imagination, always liking to make wishes. Our elders always caution that you must be careful about what you wish for, but young people sometimes just don't listen.

One girl said to the other as they lay on the ground thinking about life: "With what star up there would you like to make love?" Her friend responded, "Which ones? There are so many. Do you mean the bright white one or the bright red one?" They were silent for a while, as if in deep study, then the other said: "I'd like to sleep with the Red Star."

Her friend laughed and said: "Well, since you picked that one, the younger one, then I would like to sleep with the White Star, because he is the older one." And this is how they talked, teased, and fantasized until falling asleep.

When they awoke they found themselves in the sky world. As they looked around, they noticed the strange place and became scared, but sitting next to them were the two stars, which had become men. The White Star was very, very old and white-haired, while the younger one had strange red-colored hair. They made the girls' wish and fantasy come true, and as a result the girls ended up staying in the sky world for a long time.

As they got to know the place, they came across an old woman who sat over a hole in the sky; she sat there in deep thought, looking down. One day they asked her what she was doing, and she said: "Come and look down through this hole, down there is where you come from." And they looked down and started crying. They became very homesick.

They wished they could get down the hole and back home somehow. Each day they came by and pestered the old woman, asking if they could look down the hole. On the Earth below they could see their village, ceremonies, people happy, and medicine being made. One day the elder felt sorry for them and said: "Why don't you look

around here for some plants and roots to make a rope? Then I can help you get down with my power." The girls were very excited and they worked hard for days and nights, gathering a lot of material, cutting and pounding and shaping it into a very big rope. One day they were done and the old lady told them to get into her special basket, and she tied the long rope on the basket while singing. With her power she lowered the two girls farther and farther until they landed in an Eagle's nest.

But still they were too high and did not know how to get down from there without getting hurt. "What shall we do now?" one said. "I guess we will have to wait and holler until someone comes by to help us," replied the other, while crying. And so it came to be, until one day a Bear passed by. The girls cried out, but he ignored them. Then they taunted him: "Hey, Bear, someday you should get married. Now is your chance, help us down."

Bear thought to himself that they were not all that good-looking and perhaps would not make good wives, but he felt sorry for them and didn't want to hurt their feelings. He pretended to climb the tree and said, "I just can't get any higher," and so he went away.

The next day a Bobcat came by. The girls cried out to him for help and tried to use the same enticement. But Bobcat didn't think they were that pretty either, so he lied: "I can't climb up there, I don't have sharp enough claws," and went on his way. The following day a very ugly man came by, Wolverine. By this time the girls were getting desperate, so they said: "Hey, Wolverine, my, what a handsome and strong-looking man you are. Do you have any wives? Why don't you come up and get us? We have been waiting here just for you."

Wolverine became very excited. He thought he had finally had the good fortune to find women who appeared to appreciate what he had to offer. "They must be special to be up there so high," he said to himself as he climbed up easily. Since he could not carry both of them, it was decided that he would take one at a time. The first girl left her hair tie behind in the nest as she was being carried down. Then Wolverine went up for the second girl, who in turn also left behind one of her hair ties.

Wolverine was very happy. He carried his new wives into the forest and showed them off to everyone, all those who before had thought that he was ugly and poor.

But the girls had devised a plan. One day they said to Wolverine: "We forgot our hair ties in the nest where you found us, we must have them." Wolverine agreed to go back and get the hair ties, for he would do anything for his new wives. In the meantime, the girls pleaded with the trees for help. "We need to escape and get away from this ugly man. When he comes back to whistle for us, you help hide us and answer back by using the wind." And so it went: Every time Wolverine whistled, the wind would come up and the trees would whistle back. Wolverine still goes about doing this, hoping to someday find his two wives.

Blue Jay's Skinny Legs
(Salish-Kootnai/Flathead)

It happened a long time ago, before the first White people came into our area. There was a chief who had a very beautiful daughter. He wanted to make sure that she married a strong and healthy man. As the young men began to come around to flirt with his daughter, he became worried. He decided to reduce the odds by having a race. He informed all the young men that the one with the strongest legs could marry his daughter.

Coyote was crafty and a good runner with a lot of power, so he came first. He showed how long his legs were and how fast he could run. Then Deer came, a very handsome and strong buck. He showed how powerful his legs were at jumping, although they were somewhat knotted up. Then Grizzly Bear came along. Bear stood up and growled so everyone could see that he had very powerful and strong legs. So he claimed the girl.

But Blue Jay hollered that it was not fair, that others should still be considered. While the others were showing their legs, he hid behind an old log, where he had gathered a lot of tree moss and used clay to pack it around his legs. They looked larger and stronger than anyone's, even bigger than Grizzly Bear's. But to sweeten the pot, Blue Jay also offered all kinds of beautiful feathers he had obtained from all of his different bird relations.

The old chief was fooled by this and let his daughter go with him. Blue Jay had to carry his new wife across the stream in order to reach his tepee on the other side. As he began the hard journey, the water softened the moss and clay, so they fell from his legs.

When he climbed up on the other side of the stream bank, everyone began to laugh. Grizzly Bear came down and claimed his prize, and with his strong legs carried his new wife up the side of the mountain. Anytime he tries to come back and visit, the Blue Jay will start squawking all over the forest, and he makes a terrible noise. He does this because he is jealous and doesn't like to be laughed at.

Animal Signs and Omens

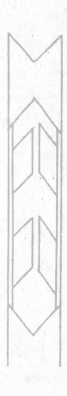

As with learning any language, to understand Nature's messages, it is first necessary to understand her symbols. Only by coming to recognize these individual symbols can we learn what she is trying to tell us.

The following list has been designed to provide you with an easy reference catalog of ancient and esoteric knowledge. It is arranged alphabetically and can be used as a sort of field guide. Thus, if you have an encounter with a certain kind of animal, you can refer to the animal section for information, or to the bird section for an explanation. This list is not complete by any means, due to the vast amount of knowledge about Nature that is recorded in Native American literature. Remember, however, that according to traditional Indian belief, animals, birds, reptiles, and all things in Nature are also "spirits," both good or bad. Hence they can represent positive or negative signs and meanings.

Antelope

▼▼▼▼▼

The Antelope serves as a messenger and forewarns us of human behavior. For example, while driving down the road you might see a herd of Antelope heading in a certain direction. This could mean that you will soon encounter a group of friendly people. If a doe comes close by, it means a friendly woman will approach; if it is a buck, it means there is a friendly man up ahead, and usually a flirtatious one. To see Antelope fighting means you will soon encounter conflict with friends or relatives. Depending upon its behavior, the Antelope can also let us know about other people's sexual feelings or desires toward us. My friend Wilson Mandan suggested I include this story here because this is how he learned the messages of the Antelope:

A long time ago, my grandpa and great-uncle were traveling back from the powwow when they saw a strange sign. My great-uncle pointed to a buck trying to mount a doe, but this was out of season and the wrong time of the year for such behavior. So he turned to my grandpa and asked, "Did you see those Antelope? I wonder what that means." At first Grandpa didn't say anything, he just got real sad. But my great-uncle kept bringing it up, knowing it was a message but not knowing what it meant. After a while Grandpa said, "Brother, we had better get to your house fast, but when we get there don't get mad."

When they got to my great-uncle's house, they caught one of his friends in bed with my great-uncle's wife. My great-uncle got very angry and almost killed the man, and he kicked his wife out. A couple of months later he saw a doe standing in his front yard. He got mad and kept trying to chase it away. It would not leave. So he went down the road to Grandpa's house and asked to borrow a rifle. Grandpa said, "What for?"

"Because there is an Antelope in my front yard and she won't leave, so I want to kill the damn thing," he responded. My grandpa looked at his younger brother sternly and said, "Don't do that. The spirits are speaking to you. A new woman will be coming to your home soon, unless you are foolish and kill the sign." His brother left the Antelope alone, and the prediction came true.

Badger

Badger is a good sign, meaning protection, but he can also warn of danger when you are traveling in a vehicle or walking. Badger medicine can be warrior medicine, doctor power, and protection power. He is courageous, tenacious, and defensive. Here is a personal experience I once had with a Badger while traveling through Oregon heading to Nevada. I was traveling down a somewhat deserted, windy country road late at night. The fog was starting to come in, which made travel difficult. I was quite some distance between towns and mainly in open range on a desert plateau. I saw a Badger sitting on the right side of the road, so I slowed down. He was looking right at me, very intently, so I brought the car to a stop and asked him: "What are you trying to tell me, little brother?" All of a sudden he started growling and pawing at the ground, as if doing a special kind of dance. So I thanked him and went on my way, watching the road carefully. A few miles later a large Bull followed by a few other cattle suddenly came charging up

77

out of a ravine, pawing their way through the snow to get up on the highway. Because I understood the omen and heeded the Badger's message, I did not get into a bad car accident. I saw the cattle just in the nick of time. I was traveling slowly and cautiously, and as a result managed to stop safely until the danger cleared. Thus, in this situation Badger came to me for protection.

Bear
▼▼▼▼▼

The Bear is always a good sign and a special power. He represents wisdom, insight, introspection, protection, and healing. If you see a Bear while hiking in the woods or along the river, then you know that a very sacred place is nearby and that the spirits of that area are checking you out. Respect the Bear and don't intimidate it, pray and give thanks to it, and make a special wish. Because of their size and temperament they can be dangerous, so don't try to approach one, either Black Bear or Grizzly. If a Bear comes to the house or around the camp in late fall looking for food, it is usually a sign that a harsh winter is coming early.

A number of years ago, my wife and I lived in a small mobile home in the woods above Trinidad, California. One day she was busy talking on the telephone and noticed that our youngest child, Wind-Wolf, who at that time was about one and a half years old, had crawled out on the front porch and was screaming. She went out to get him and suddenly noticed a large Bobcat standing in front of our son, hissing and lashing out at the toddler with his claws. He was just about ready to pounce on him when my wife acted swiftly. She literally kicked the Bobcat off the porch, grabbed the child, ran back into the house, and closed the door. Although she was scared and shaking, she did manage to get the smudge bowl, burn cedar and angelica root, and pray over the child for protection. The Bobcat climbed on the roof, tried getting into windows via tree branches around the trailer, and occasionally even got brave enough to scratch and pound on the door.

My wife was afraid to leave the house, so she called me at work and asked for advice and help. It was during early winter and turning dark outside, so I left immediately and began the thirty-mile drive along the coast toward home. I stopped at a sacred place called Strawberry Rock and prayed for my family, especially my child, because this was a bad sign that a jealous or evil person with power had sent their spirit ally against my family. By the time I got home and pulled up into the driveway, I could see a young Black Bear fighting with the Bobcat. I stayed in my car and watched until the Bobcat was chased away. The Bear hung around our place for four days, during which time our child developed a very bad cold and fever. But by the fourth day the child was well and the Bear was gone.

Last year another Indian family, living in a city, was not so fortunate. According to national news reports and the local newspaper, a Mountain Lion attacked their four-year-old son, mauled it to death, and was chased down by the family and neighbors before it would let go of the child. This happened in northern Montana in 1991, and rumor has it that the family is still having strange problems. Occurrences like this one are neither a coincidence nor simply an accident. They are Nature's way of communicating to us. Such things are indeed out of the ordinary. Unless the animal has rabies or is wounded and provoked, or used as a source of power in a negative way, it normally does not behave like that.

For a better understanding of Bears, I would suggest reading *Giving Voice to Bear*, by David Rockwell, and "Digging for Medicine: Bears in Native American Healing Traditions," also by David Rockwell.

Beaver

▼▼▼▼▼

Beaver can have multiple meanings as a sign. He is a good power but can warn that confusion and conflict are forthcoming if he settles in around one's camp or home. He is industrious, hardworking, intelligent, but also selfish. He is determined to finish his own tasks, such as constructing houses, clearing trees, and building dams that will flood the area.

There is an old Indian story I heard about "Beaver and Porcupine" from a friend of mine, Brown Bear Mallot, a spiritual leader from the Tlingit tribe in Alaska:

A long time ago, Beaver and Porcupine were great friends and they went everywhere together. The Porcupine often visited the Beaver's house, but the Beaver did not like him to visit because he always left behind sharp quills.

One time the Porcupine said he wanted to go out to the Beaver's house for a visit and to eat some different trees. The Beaver said, "OK, get on my back and I will take you across the water." So he started with Porcupine on his back, but instead of heading toward the house, he headed out toward deeper water, out in the middle of the lake. Then he just dumped him there, on an old stump, hoping he would sink.

The Porcupine got scared at first, but then he decided to sing his power song. He sang something like "Let it become frozen, let it become solid ice, then I can walk and not sink." And he sang some more, "Let me be able to walk to Wolverine's place," meaning he wanted to walk ashore on water (ice).

So as soon as he sang his song, the cold north wind came in and the lake froze, and then he walked home. Later the two friends met again and started playing together. Porcupine said, "You come now, it is my turn to take you on my back for a ride." Reluctantly, the Beaver got on Porcupine's back, and the Porcupine took him to the top of a very high tree and left him there. For a long time the Beaver did not know what to do or how to get down. Finally, he got up the courage to try and walk down, using his sharp teeth to make notches, like the rungs of a ladder. To this day you can still see notches all over different kinds of trees. Beaver did this just in case he ever gets stuck up in a tree again.

Bobcat and Panther

Bobcat and Panther (Mountain Lion) are bad signs. To see one means you are being stalked, physically or spiritually, by an enemy. On the other hand, Bobcat and Panther are good hunters and protectors. Their power and medicine can be used for good luck and skill in hunting, or for protection against other powers and people. Here is a story my father-in-law, Chuck Donahue, told me:

Panther lived over there inside Redwood Creek, with two young boys, Bobcat and Fox. He used to go out hunting every morning, and sometimes he would use a Deer's head for a decoy. Every day he would tell the boys: "Do not go up that hill over there." He would always tell them that, and then go hunting.

He always returned and brought back Deer. He cut it up and didn't waste anything. The house was full of meat and hides.

But the two boys wanted to be like Panther. Bobcat and Fox said one day, "Why does he always tell us that? Why can't we go up that hill and hunt like him?" So they decided to go.

They went up the steep hill and came to where a Grizzly Bear was living. They teased him and tried to provoke him into a fight.

In the meantime, Panther came home from hunting and found his house smashed and all the food gone. Bobcat and Fox were also gone. There was Bear dung everywhere, and Panther decided to get even with Grizzly Bear. He started off, stalking, up the hill. Then he saw smoke coming from an old house. He stopped and peeked inside. He saw a man, Grizzly Bear, lying by the fire and a woman sitting nearby eating.

He shot the man in his shoulder as he lay asleep. Suddenly the old man woke up and growled, "What did you put in that fire, woman, to make it pop and snap so much?"

"That was not the fire," she growled back. "Don't you know you have been shot?" Panther continued shooting; he shot a lot of arrows into the old Grizzly Bear. "You can't kill him that way," the bear's wife said, laughing. "His heart is in his foot."

So Panther tried again, this time shooting the Grizzly Bear in his foot, and killed him.

Panther went back to his house and rebuilt it. He took the two boys and pushed them into the fire. "What did I tell you boys?" he hollered. "Didn't I tell you not to go up the hill?"

The boys were scared, so they went outside and hid in the dark, hoping that Panther wouldn't find them. But Panther is a good stalker; he found them and brought them back to the house. After that, he took good care of them because he is also a good protector.

Later, while out hunting, he saw Grizzly Bear again. He said, "I thought I had killed you." Ever since then, you will not find Panther and Grizzly Bear together; if you do, it is a bad sign.

Buffalo/Bison

The Buffalo is a good sign, a strong power, and a special messenger of strength and survival to the Plains tribes. The very essence of the Plains culture, their survival, their religion, their way of life, and the basis of their spirituality was predicated upon the Buffalo. Western exploiters almost made this magnificent animal extinct. But Chief Yellowtail of the Crow Indian Nation helped bring it back. Prior to European invasion it is estimated that there were over sixty million buffalo on the North American continent. Within one hundred years the vast herds that had once roamed free were reduced to a small number. The survivors went to Yellowstone National Park for preservation, while the Crow Indians tried to save some because they considered the animal so sacred. The White Bison is especially sacred, symbolically representing high spirituality, wisdom, and wealth. There is an ancient Sioux (Lakota-Dakota-Brule) legend about White Buffalo Calf Woman, who introduced to the Native people the sacred pipe and special ceremonies and rituals for their tribe (refer to John Neihardt's *Black Elk Speaks* and Richard Erdoes and John Lame Deer's *Lame Deer Seeker of Visions* for a detailed description).

Coyote
▼▼▼▼▼

Coyote is one of the most ancient mythic symbols for most Native tribes. He is often portrayed as either the creator or the trickster. He is full of magic, special powers, and teachings. We learn from the lessons that Coyote gives us about the mistakes and/or accomplishments he has made in life. Depending upon the circumstance or situation in your life, the sign of Coyote is usually a good sign, but beware, it can also be misleading. This omen, or sign, always requires careful study and can change from time to time, from person to person, and from situation to situation. Here is an ancient story I heard from my Okanogan/Lake Band friend, Glen Raymond. It is a "Coyote story" that tells how Coyote got his name and special power:

In the Beginning of the world, the Great Spirit called a council meeting of all the Animal people. He said: "Some of you do not have names yet, and some of you do not like the names you have now. So tomorrow, before the sun rises, I will give a name to everyone. And I will also give each person a special arrow."

This caused a big uproar and chattering, but the Great Creator continued. "Come to my lodge as soon as the darkness is gone. The one who gets here first can choose any name he wants. And I will give him the longest arrow, and that power symbol will mean he has the most power."

As everyone was leaving the meeting, Coyote turned and said to his friend the Fox: "I don't like my name, so I am going to make sure I am there first. I think I would like to be called Grizzly Bear or Eagle."

Fox just laughed and laughed. "Nobody wants your name. I think you'll probably have to keep it," he said.

"No!" said Coyote. "I'll prove it to you. Just wait and see. I'll be there first. I won't even go to sleep tonight just to make sure."

That night he sat by his fire and stayed awake for a long time. Owl hooted at him, making him feel nervous. Frog croaked in the marshes and sang songs that made Coyote sleepy. Coyote heard all the animals, even the Crickets. He kept staring at the sky, and soon even the stars began to slowly disappear, making his eyelids feel heavier and heavier. He became very sleepy.

Suddenly he jumped up and said: "I've got to do something about this!" So he looked around, found two sticks, and propped them under his eyelids. "Now I can stay awake," he said to himself.

But soon he was fast asleep. When he did finally wake up, the sun was already passing over the mountains, and Coyote's eyes were dry from having been propped up all night. And even though his eyes were sore and he could hardly see, he ran as fast as he could to the Great Creator's lodge. It was empty except for the Great Creator.

"I want to be Grizzly Bear," he screamed, thinking he was the very first one there. The Great Creator responded: "That name is already taken, and Grizzly Bear has the longest arrow. He will be chief and medicine man of all the animals on Earth."

"Then I will be Eagle," said Coyote firmly. "That name has also been taken," said the Great Creator. "And Eagle has the second-longest arrow."

Coyote became frustrated and worried. "Then I will be Salmon," he cried sadly. "That name has also been taken, and Salmon has the third arrow," said the Great Creator. "So he will be chief of all the Fish people. Only the shortest arrow is left, and it has only one name on it. Here, take it," said the Great Creator.

Coyote sank down by the sacred fire in despair. His eyes were still sore and dry, he couldn't even cry. So the Great Creator put water in them. Coyote sat and thought about his predicament.

"I know," he said, jumping up. "I will ask Grizzly Bear to change names with me." And off he went. "No, no, no," said Grizzly Bear. "I cannot do this for you because the Great Creator gave me this sacred name."

Coyote returned to the fire and thought some more. "Then I will go look for Eagle. But how can I fly? I know! I will go look for Salmon. But how can I swim?" He was so sad and disgusted he began to cry.

The Great Creator heard him and came out of the lodge. He said: "Don't feel so bad, Coyote. I have a special power for you. I wanted you to be the last one to come because I have special work for you to do, and you will need a special power and ability to do it. Now study your arrow and gift. With it you can change yourself into any form. And when you or someone else needs special help, call upon your power.

"And lastly, Fox will be your little brother and messenger. He will help you when you need assistance in your work. If you die, he will have the power to bring you back to life again. Now go throughout the world and be a teacher."

That is how Coyote got his name and special power; he teaches us about the powers of Nature, behavior, and values.

Deer

▼▼▼▼▼

Deer are good powers and can be messengers in many different ways. They can be our eyes and ears if we acquire their power. They can tell us what is up ahead on the road while we are traveling, help us see into the future via dreams and meditation, and remind us that we should try to live lives that are balanced and graceful. If a woman sees a buck while traveling, it is a warning that she might meet a man up ahead who has sexual desire for her. And more than likely he will be flirtatious. This can be a good sign or a bad sign, depending upon one's personal desires and perspective. By the same token, if a man sees a doe alongside the road, it is usually a sign that he will encounter a sensuous and flirtatious woman, a woman who would like to mate with him. Once again the sign can be good or bad, depending upon one's ethics, desires, or preference.

If you go on a vision quest and see a Deer along the way, it is usually an indication that you will meet a stranger on the trail, so study the Deer's behavior well. More than one Deer means more than one man or woman. If the Deer comes close to your campfire and hangs around, it is trying to bring you a message from the spirit world. Thank it for coming and ask it to talk to you in a dream, in a language you can understand. I provide a detailed example and experience of such a situation in my book *Native Healer*. If a man sees a big buck pawing the ground with its head bent downward, then it is a sign that he will encounter a challenger in a social situation involving women.

Elk

▼▼▼▼▼

The message of the Elk is similar to that of Deer, but the Elk is also a strong protector of women. If women need special protection or help,

they should make prayers to the Elk or consult with an Elk medicine man. The power and spirit of the Elk can help women with female problems, fear, anxiety, sexual problems, and bad luck. So it is a good sign if a woman sees an Elk in the wild. More information about Elk medicine can be found in Richard Erdoes and John Lame Deer's book, *Lame Deer Seeker of Visions*, or in Erdoes and my friend Archie Fire Lame Deer's book, *The Path of Power*, and Joseph E. Brown's recent book entitled *Animals of the Soul*.

Fox

Fox is a bad sign, a messenger of danger, sickness, or possible death, but he is also a good power and a guardian. Certain shamans can use the power and spirit of the Fox to reverse a problem, as in the case of bringing someone out of a coma or back to life after the person has been pronounced dead. The Fox is clever, intelligent, a good hunter, and a wise friend. He also represents pride, regality, and loyalty.

Gopher

Gopher is a bad sign but a good animal. Some Native tribes such as the Shoshone believe he is a doctor and can help take away sickness if you go to his hole, make an offering, and ask for help. If he comes up out of the hole and digs around, that means he is taking your sickness, pain, or disease away. Other tribes, like the Yurok, Karuk, and Hupa in northwestern California, believe the Gopher is a messenger of death. If you see him digging a hole in the yard near the house, it is a sign that someone you know will die soon. The Gopher is showing you that a person's grave is being dug. The closer the hole to the front door of the house, the closer this person is to your family. A Gopher digging a hole in the garden simply means that he is hungry. If he becomes a pest, try to offer him food and make an agreement with him not to bother the rest of your garden.

Mink
▼▼▼▼▼

Mink's message is similar to those of Otter and Muskrat; he is a good sign and a good power, and sometimes a symbol of wealth and good health. He represents good behavior because he is good-natured, healthy, and playful. If you see a Mink nearby when you are fishing, it is a sign that you will have good luck when fishing. Mink's power is used in Indian gambling hand games in northwestern California, and his fur is highly prized for ceremonial regalia, status, and recognition. Here is an ancient story that Rudolph Socktish, the Hupa ceremonial leader, once told me:

A long time ago, Mink heard that there was a big gambling game going on over on the coast. He decided he would freshen up for the event by first playing a few hand games here at Hupa. He didn't do so well and lost just about everything he had. So he started walking through Redwood Creek, hoping to find some peace and quiet to think about his predicament.

He was very tired, and halfway through the ancient redwood forest he decided to build a fire and cook some dinner. It seemed as though nothing would go right for him. He tried catching fish but had no luck. He even had a difficult time getting the campfire going because the wood was too wet. Eventually he fell asleep.

Then a strange thing happened. That night he had a dream, and he thought he heard a good-luck gambling song. He woke up in the middle of the night and looked around but couldn't see anything. The

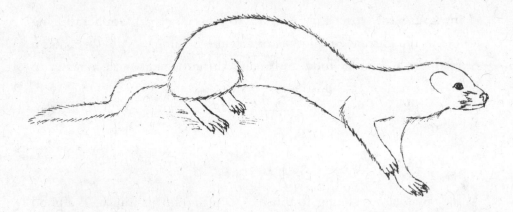

fog was too thick. But he faintly heard someone singing from the creek. He strained his eyes but still couldn't see who it was. He put dry pinecones on the fire to make more light but still couldn't see anything. After a while he got sleepy and fell asleep.

The next morning a large Woodpecker came by looking for breakfast. It started pecking on the tall Douglas fir tree that Mink was sleeping under. It pecked so hard it knocked a large fir bough into the campfire, which in turn sent a lot of smoke all over Mink. He woke up from all the disturbance and began to choke and stumble in the smoke. Half awake and half scared, he fell into the creek and got caught up in the waterfall. The swift water carried him all the way down to the Pacific Coast, right to the big gambling game.

The people there saw Mink and asked him to come and play. "I have nothing of value to bet," he said sadly. "Then bet that beautiful hide you are wearing," the others said. Mink sat down and tried to think of a powerful song. Soon he heard the woodpecker, and then he remembered the song from the waterfall and sang it. He won a lot of wealth that way.

Muskrat
▼▼▼▼▼

Muskrat is also a good sign. He is considered sacred to the Iroquois Six Nations because Muskrat helped create the Earth. He is industrious and a critical thinker, and represents wealth.

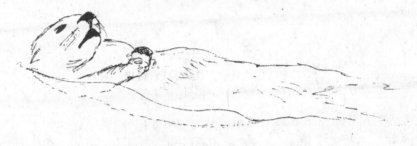

Otter
▼▼▼▼▼

Otter is a good sign. He represents wealth, playfulness, and happiness, and also brings good luck and good health. His message is similar to Mink's. Native men and women in a variety of different tribes often used Otter and Mink skins for hair ties and decorative hair wrappings. They are symbols of good luck, beauty, and wealth.

Porcupine
▼▼▼▼▼▼

Porcupine, a good sign, usually brings messages about the weather or about hunting. My friend Tony Gall, who is a Pit River Indian from California, told me that every time he sees a Porcupine when he is hunting, it is a good sign that he will see and kill a Deer. My friend Darryl Wilson from Pit River said the Porcupine warns about weather changes. For example, if a person sees a Porcupine close to the house during late fall, it is a warning that an early winter will come in on a cold wind.

Porpoise/Dolphin

▼▼▼▼▼▼▼▼▼▼▼

These animals are good signs and very good powers. To see a Porpoise near the shore is a good sign, meaning good luck or protection is coming. The elders who live by the ocean say, "If someone is sick in your family, or if you are having bad luck, or if someone is threatening you, then go to the ocean and make prayers to the Porpoise. Tell it what you want or need, ask it for help. If he stands up and laughs, then dances backwards, your wish will come true."

I have talked to older Indian men who were in the Navy during World War II and they have told me stories about how the Dolphins saved their lives. In one situation a pilot was shot down and under attack in the water by Sharks. He prayed and asked the Great Creator for help. Shortly after he sang his song the Dolphins came in and chased away the Sharks. They pushed him all the way to shore. In another story an Indian fisherman's boat caught on fire and he had to jump into the ocean. Once again the Sharks came in just before this happened (a bad omen and a forewarning); then they waited while he desperately tried to swim to safety. He said the Porpoises came in and formed a circle of protection around him until another boat came up and pulled him out of the water. For some Native tribes, it is also a good sign to see a school of dolphins or porpoises come by during fishing season. It means the fish runs will be prosperous.

Raccoon

▼▼▼▼▼

Raccoon is a good sign. He is a good protector. He is intelligent, cunning, clean, and very helpful. If you don't know how to do something, then make prayers and a wish to the Raccoon, leave him some food, and he will show you how to resolve your problem. The Raccoon can also be used as a doctor power, hunting power, and protection power. If you ever get lost in the woods or out in Nature, just ask the Raccoon to help. He likes helping people.

Shark

▼▼▼▼▼

Sharks are bad signs and warn of danger. If a large school of Sharks start coming too close to shore, it is a sign that an earthquake, tidal wave, or hurricane is coming. Sharks do not belong up freshwater rivers, so the rare appearance of Sharks up a river is a warning that a very bad flood is forthcoming. In the late 1970s my wife Tela's cousins, the Maasts brothers from Klamath, caught a Great White Shark in their traditional Indian gill net about nine miles up the Klamath River. The incident appeared on national news because it caused such a commo-

tion. It was a very unusual occurrence. Auntie Geneve Maasts told her boys not to eat the Shark because it was a bad sign. A couple of weeks later we had floods and a 7.8-magnitude earthquake in our area.

Shrew and Mole

The Shrew and the Mole, although somewhat different, are both considered bad powers and bad signs. A Shrew should never come into the house; if it does, it is a sign that someone really hates your family and they will do whatever is necessary to bring serious harm to your family. They are vicious and vindictive little creatures who will stop at nothing in order to get what they want. They are quiet, sneaky, fast, and very good listeners. A mole seen digging around the front or back yard is usually a messenger of death. His symbolic action is saying: "Hey, look at me, I am already digging a grave for your friend or family member."

Skunk

The Skunk is a bad sign and a bad power. The sorcerers work with this power and send it as an ally against people to cause conflict, sickness, and bad luck. A Skunk is usually a sign that evil is around you and that every effort should be made to pray against it. Here is an old story I once heard about Skunk that was told to me by Isadore Tom, an elderly medicine man from the Lummi tribe in northwestern Washington.

A long time ago, there was a Skunk who decided to live near the village of the people. He was sent by a jealous shaman from a neighboring tribe. The Skunk was lazy and preferred to steal food rather than work on his own for it. He had a special power that could be used to chase people away if they tried to stop him from stealing the food.

When angered, he could produce an odor that was capable of killing his enemy. According to legend, he got this poisonous gas from a mineral spring in Nature, a bad place, and he kept the location secret for generations.

One day a group of people from the village tried to chase the Skunk away because they didn't want him stealing food and bullying everyone around. They became frightened and ran to the top of a hill, and they figured the Skunk would probably chase them. But they already had a plan.

They got a large rock, prayed on it, and heated it up in a fire. They planned to roll it down upon the Skunk in the hope of destroying him. The skunk became so mad and aggressive that he didn't even notice what the people were up to, so he came charging up the hill. When the people thought he was close enough, they got a large stick and pushed the hot rock over the edge. It rolled down over the Skunk and burned him, knocking most of the poisonous power and smell out of him. It did not kill the Skunk, but it did break his medicine. And that is why today he can't kill people with his smell. That is also why he has a stripe down the middle of his back. That stripe now acts as a warning to anyone who might confuse the Skunk with Fisher or Wolverine.

Weasel

Weasel is a good sign. This animal is cunning, playful, smart, swift, and very courageous. He is a good friend, protector, and adviser. He is also considered good luck. Among the Karuk Indians of northwestern California, the Weasel is considered a teacher and protector. There are many stories about Weasel outwitting witches and serving as a cru-

sader against the evil actions of those who are jealous, wicked, and mean. Weasel is a power and animal ally called upon to protect oneself and one's family against the challenges and attacks of sorcerers. My father, Charles "Red Hawk" Thom, told me this story:

A long time ago, a man lived over at Hupa, near the Trinity River. He liked to gamble but was not so lucky. One day he lost everything at the handstick game, and on the way home sat down by the river and cried. He was destitute and afraid to tell his wife that he had also lost her in the gambling game.

That night he fell asleep. He thought he heard something running around. He could hardly see it because it was so fast. He tried to catch it but it was too fast, and yet it kept pestering him. He must have spent hours trying to catch the little animal, just to see what it was. Finally, he gave up and started crying again. At last, Weasel came out of a hole, from under the roots of a large tree, and he was singing. His fur was slick and beautiful. He told the man, "I feel sorry for you. Listen to my song and learn it and you will always be lucky. Here, use my hide for your gambling sticks and I will bring you good luck, I will be your adviser." After that, anytime the Hupa man saw a Weasel on the way to the hand games, he knew he would be lucky. In fact, many years later he ended up with numerous wives.

Whale

▼▼▼▼▼

The sign of the Whale can be very confusing at times. In northwestern California, for example, and for some tribes up along the Pacific Northwest Coast, the Whale is a sign of wealth and prosperity. It is considered a good sign to see one out in the ocean, near the coast. Thus, many tribal groups performed a welcome ceremony for the Whale when they saw it near the rocky coastline. They would offer it tobacco and food, such as acorn soup, and make a wish to it for good luck and wealth. To see a Whale go up a freshwater river, however, is a bad sign. This tells the people that things are out of balance with Nature, and it is usually a warning that floods or bad earthquakes are forthcoming. (Remember the large Whale that got stuck up the Sacramento River in California a few years back? Droughts then came, followed by floods.)

To see Whales ramming themselves up on the beach is a bad sign from Nature. It usually means that a tidal wave or hurricane is forthcoming. This happened a number of times on the East Coast along the Atlantic Ocean. Some of the elders carry the message a step further and say: "When large schools of Whales keep running up on the shore, it is a sign that they are trying to become land creatures once again; hence it is a sign and warning that the Earth may be preparing for a complete rotation of its axis. Thus, the tribes should begin plans to move inland, to higher ground, for protection, and begin to store food and supplies for survival, allowing up to a decade for preparation."

Wolf

▼▼▼▼▼

Wolves almost became extinct in this country because of the European fear and hatred of this animal. But the Native American people have

97

historically had high regard for Wolves. The Wolf is considered a good sign, a protector, a good hunter, wise, cunning, intelligent, strong, gregarious, courageous, and yet mysterious. Although Western people have perpetuated a stereotype that Wolves attack and kill people, even eat them, such has not been the case in Native mythology and lore. Shamans and warriors drew their symbolic and spiritual power from the Wolf. Some tribes even had Wolf clans, Wolf societies, and Wolf ceremonial dances in recognition of the sacredness of this animal. A Kiowa Indian friend told me this ancient story about the Wolves:

A long time ago, our people were out camping. There was a young man, his wife, and his brother. They set out by themselves to look for game. This young man would leave his younger brother and his wife in camp and go out to look for Deer. Every time his brother would leave, the boy would go to a high hill nearby and sit there all day until his older brother returned. One time, before the boy went as usual to the hill, his sister-in-law said, "Why are you so lonesome all the time? Can we be sweethearts?" The boy answered, "No, I love and respect my brother and I would not want to hurt him that way." But the woman was persistent. "Your brother wouldn't even know. You and I could keep it a secret. Come and sleep with me and I will make you happy. Don't worry, your brother will never find out."

The younger boy stood steadfast in his response. "No!" he repeated, "I cannot do that." One night, as they all went to sleep, the young woman went to where the boy used to sit on the hill. She began to dig. She dug a deep hole so that no one would ever hear him. Then she covered it by placing a hide over the hole, and she made it look natural so that nobody would notice it. She went back to the camp and lay down.

The next day the older brother went hunting and the younger brother went to where he usually sat. The young woman watched him and saw him drop out of sight. She went up the hill and looked into the pit and said, "I guess you will want to make love to me now. If you are willing to be my sweetheart, I will let you out. If not, you will have to stay in there until you die."

Still the boy persisted and said no. After a while the hunter returned and asked his wife if she had seen his brother. She said, "No, but I think he went up there on the hill."

That night, after bedding down, the older brother turned and said to his wife, "I think I hear someone hollering for help. Could it be my brother?" His wife looked up and responded, "No, I think it is only Wolves up on the hill, up there."

But the older brother did not sleep well that night. He said to his wife, "You must have scolded him to make him go. He probably went home angry and hurt." She replied, "I did not say anything to him. Every day when you go hunting he goes to that hill." The next day they broke camp to see if he was over there; but they could not find him. The brother was sad and felt that his younger brother had died somehow. The mother and father of the boy also cried when they heard the bad news.

In the meantime, the boy in the pit was afraid and crying, and he was also very hungry. He looked up and saw something; it was a Wolf trying to pull off the Deer hide. He said to the boy, "Why are you down there?"

The boy told the Wolf what had happened, that his sister-in-law had done this to him. The Wolf felt sorry for the boy and told him, "I will get you out. If I get you out, you will become my son, OK?" Then the boy looked up again and he heard more Wolves howling; there was a whole pack of them. They all pitched in and started digging to help him get out of the hole. Soon he got out.

It was very cold that night. Once again the Wolves felt sorry for the boy, so they laid beside him and kept him warm. The next morning the Wolves asked the boy what he ate. He told them he liked meat. So the Wolves went out and killed a weak, young Buffalo and brought it to him. But the boy had nothing to butcher it with. They decided to tear the Buffalo calf into separate pieces. The boy then ate until he was full. In the meantime, the older Wolf asked the other Wolves if they knew where a flint knife could be found, and one of them said he had seen a knife on the trail. They gave it to the boy, and after that, he could butcher his own meat every time they went out hunting for him.

Sometime after that, a man from the camp was out hunting. He saw a pack of Wolves with a man. He rode up to see who such a man was, but he could not recognize the man running with Wolves. Later the hunter returned to camp and told the people. The council thought about the strange sign and decided it might be the young boy who had gotten lost sometime before.

At another time the Buffalo herd had been slaughtered and there was plenty of meat stored up for the winter. So some of the younger men decided to go out and kill some Wolves for their hides. It was at this time that they noticed a man running with a Wolf pack. Finding it strange, they came back and told the elders' council. It was decided that the whole camp would go and see for themselves. They saw the young man and kept chasing him and the pack until they all got tired and could not go any farther. The young man acted like a Wolf, he growled at them like a Wolf, and he even tried to bite them like a Wolf when they tried to tie him up.

All this time the Wolf pack kept howling around the camp. The elders asked the young man what had happened to him; he told his mother and father. Then he asked if he could be set free to go and talk to his father Wolf, because their howling meant something special. At first the people did not want to set the young man free; the parents were afraid that he would try to run off again. But they let him go. He went straight to the Wolf pack and sat down and talked to them. Then he came back to camp. He told the elders that the wolf elders demanded a replacement for him. The Indian people would be required to never kill a Wolf without just cause and proper prayer payment. In return, the Wolves would always bring special messages to the people, for example, where to find game when hunting, and through their actions teach them how to live and survive.

Wolverine and Fisher

Wolverine and Fisher are good omens, and signs of good luck and wealth. Their power and medicine can be used for warrior power and provide good protection. They are good animals to have around outside the house. If a person is getting ready to go gambling and they see a Wolverine, Fisher, Otter, or Mink, then it is a good-luck omen that they will be lucky and win.

Bird Signs and Omens

All cultures have ancient myths and stories about birds serving as messengers and omens to human beings. The Egyptians, for example, have the Falcon. The Bible tells a story about Noah, the Great Flood, and the Dove that was sent to find dry land; the English have the legend about Ravens surrounding the Queen's Palace; Muhammad and the White Hawk. Thus, what follows here is a list of birds and their symbolic meanings as I have come to understand them.

Blue Jay/Stellar Jay

Jays are beautifully colored birds, but they have bad power. They warn us about the kind of people we will soon see; they are challengers and negative entities. Sorcerers use the Blue Jay as a source of bad power. Blue Jays gossip and are noisy, arrogant, prideful, and selfish. They steal, lie, and cheat. They are lazy and take from others for their own purposes and desires. If seen around the house, a Jay can be a sign that jealous and evil people are praying against you in a bad way.

Here is an old Blue Jay story I heard from my dad, Charlie Thom, who is a medicine man from the Karuk tribe in northwestern California:

You know, all birds have a special kind of power, and we use these powers and their colors in our sacred dances, rituals, and for healing. Not all colors that are considered the most beautiful necessarily mean that that bird is the most powerful or the best kind of bird. For example, a long time ago everyone thought that Blue Jay, with her most beautiful blue color of the sky, was the prettiest. So they looked up to her as a doctor, thinking she must have gotten her power from the sky. But she was mean, she cussed a lot, she liked to spread lies and gossip. Even worse, she used her powers to make people sick. Then she would charge the sick person a lot of money to use her power to make them well. In this way she would actually be taking back her own power. But everyone thought she was a doctor and went to her for help.

One day she was running around busy talking too much when she should have been storing up her acorns and hazelnuts for the oncoming winter. All the signs in Nature were warning that an early winter was coming, but still she paid no attention. Gray Squirrel and Chipmunk worked hard all day gathering and storing their food in the old trees. She tried to get them to talk and visit, but they refused, concerning themselves more with surviving the winter.

So Blue Jay got mad and shot a worm into Chipmunk. Down he went, crying and hollering in pain. He hollered so much that everyone in the forest came to see what the problem was. Blue Jay came also. She said: "I am a doctor; I can sing and dance on you. I can suck out

the sickness, but it is going to cost you a lot of money—most of your acorns." By evil tricks such as this, she had figured out an easy way to get her own food stored up for the winter.

So she sang and danced, flashed all her beautiful colors, and in a very secretive and sneaky manner pulled out her own bad power from Chipmunk. She sucked it out of him, and showed the worm in her hand to everyone. She said: "Other people who you think are your friends are doing this to you. They are jealous; they were wishing you would die so they could have your food cache." Chipmunk became well, while Blue Jay went home with her bounty.

Then a couple of weeks went by and Blue Jay noticed that her supply was getting low. The first sign of cold weather and possible snow was coming into the forest. She looked around, but most of the other birds and animals were gone. Then she saw Chipmunk and thought: "I know he has lots of food hidden. I will make him give me all his wealth." Once again she sang her devil song and caused Chipmunk to get sick. But this time he really was dying because she had used too much power.

Chipmunk called to his cousin Gray Squirrel and pleaded with him to go get Blue Jay. "Offer her anything," he said. "Tell her I don't want to die. Tell her I will give anything to live." So they summoned Blue Jay. She said: "You are really in bad shape this time. I don't think you are going to live, so it is going to cost you a lot more this time for me to try to save you." Then they paid her with all the hazelnuts and acorns that were left.

Afterward it happened again. Chipmunk got very, very ill. But his friends became suspicious; one of them said: "Perhaps we should find another doctor, someone from a long ways off." About that time Hummingbird and Flickerbird came by. Hummingbird was traveling long-distance, heading south to warmer weather. They heard Chipmunk crying and felt sorry for him. They both sang and danced on him. Flickerbird used her Fire power to burn the sickness out while Hummingbird sucked the poison out. Then Flickerbird, who was a good seer, said: "The fire will throw this bad sickness back to where it came from. Then you will know who really did it. What goes around comes around; that is ancient law." They heard a horrible squawking noise, then a crash. It was Blue Jay, who fell from the tree, sick and hollering. Hummingbird said: "It was Blue Jay who did it; there is your truth." Then they all knew it. Flickerbird and Hummingbird did not demand payment for their services; they were happy to see Chipmunk get well and stay well. And this is how it has been ever since, so choose your doctors wisely.

Buzzard
▼▼▼▼▼

Buzzards and Vultures are bad signs. They are messengers who warn us of interruptions or problems forthcoming. While traveling to San Francisco, I saw a number of Buzzards come flying in on different sides of the road; sometimes they crisscrossed back and forth. I knew that they were trying to warn me of road construction ahead, barriers and problems, or the possibility of pedestrians, bike riders, or animals in the road. One time I was leaving my house to catch a plane and I made prayers for protection to the sky for the airplane, and was just warming up the car and getting ready to head for the airport. Suddenly a flock of Buzzards came in and began to circle over my house, and then the car, and then they went out toward the airport. I couldn't figure out what they were trying to say at first, so I prayed and talked to them. I offered them tobacco. Immediately afterward a large Buzzard landed on the roof of the house with a bag in his beak. Then it dawned on me to check my luggage. I had forgotten it and left it in the house while rustling around to catch a plane on time!

Another time I was in Nevada and heading toward a Native spiritual gathering in Susanville, California. Approximately twenty miles out of town, I saw a group of Buzzards on the side of the road eating and fighting with one another. I knew it was a warning to be careful of the food up ahead. So once again I prayed to the Great Spirit, burned and offered my sacred angelica root to the Buzzards as a gesture of thanks, and went to the meeting/gathering. I did not eat the food, despite the fact that this meant I was violating Indian custom and law (according to tribal custom, a guest should always eat food when offered; otherwise it is an insult). I found out later that a lot of people got sick from eating a spoiled turkey.

Another time I took my children swimming on a hot day to a spot on the river outside Spokane, Washington. We were all walking barefoot over rocks, heading toward a more sandy spot. Suddenly a Buzzard swooped down and flew directly over the nice spot we intended to use, so I told the children to avoid it and pick a different place, which they grudgingly did. Shortly afterward another family came and went directly to the sandy place we had originally picked out. Once again the Buzzard flew in, but they ignored it. As they proceeded to spread out the blanket and get settled in, chaos erupted. One of the children cut his foot badly on a broken beer bottle, the mother stepped in dog feces and was cussing about it, the father unearthed a dead dog under his large towel while trying to rearrange the spot for comfort, and the other child almost drowned in the swift but hidden undertow of the river current directly in front of them. I was certainly glad I had known Nature's secret language system!

Here is an old story about Buzzard that one of my mentors, Calvin Rube, an Indian doctor from the Yurok tribe in northwestern California, told me:

A long, long time ago, Buzzard traveled all over the world. He was constantly eating. Sometimes he ate so much he got too fat to fly, so he would just sit around on the tree branches and sleep with his head hanging down. The other birds would never visit with Buzzard because they thought he was too mean and grouchy, and sometimes because he stank too much. That is why they never invited him to sing and dance in their ceremonies either.

Buzzard used to brag a lot, too. He told the other birds: "I can eat anything in the world. You other birds can only eat certain things. Some of you can only eat seeds, berries, fish, or fresh-killed meat. Not me, I can eat anything at any time, and I can eat more than any of you!"

Blue Jay got tired of hearing Buzzard brag so much. One day she told the other birds: "Did you ever notice how he is a bad sign? Every time you see him there is something dead lying around. And he is always trying to interfere in something, always causing an interruption somewhere."

"Yeah, that's right," said some of the other birds, like Robin, Flickerbird, Meadowlark, and Quail. Then Blue Jay continued: "He thinks he's so great just because he is bigger than us, can fly higher, and eats more. Besides, he never shares. But I think he is ugly and stinks. I am going to make a curse on him to teach him a lesson. I wish he would get fat, bald, old, and wrinkly-looking. And I hope he gets bad bellyaches from eating too much."

One day Buzzard was flying around eating everything in sight. He wouldn't even let the other Buzzards have a bite to eat. He ate dead animals whenever he saw them. He ate poisonous snakes, scratchy bugs, smelly dead fish, and even a dead human. Buzzard ate so much that he didn't even bother to clean his head, take a bath, or anything; he just kept flying around in circles, looking, watching, waiting for something else to eat, dead or alive.

One day in summer it got really hot. Buzzard got so sick that all he could do was sit on the side of the riverbank, on an old log, and moan. He was stuffed, too fat to fly into a shady tree. He was too sick to

holler for help, and too weak to clean himself. All the dead meat left on his head began to rot in the hot sun. He stank so bad that nobody in Nature would help him. Within a few days his feathers fell out and the hot sun burned his scalp red all the way down to his neck.

Buzzard was so sick he started to die. All he could do was moan and cry, and still nobody came to help him. But on the fourth day he heard someone try to talk. He looked all around and saw this little plant just below him. The happy little green plant was singing and swaying in the warm summer breeze. She said: "Hey, you sick bird, I can help you. I can heal anybody; that is my job. Just reach down here and take a few bites of my leaves, chew them up real good, then swallow my power into your rotten belly."

It was all Buzzard could do to bend over, but that is what he did. He said: "I don't have much to offer but a few of my feathers. Maybe they can keep you warm from the morning dew. Here, I'll trade you for your medicine." So he reached down and took the herb. After a while he got well again. Before leaving, he said: "Thank you for helping me. I will never forget you because your medicine is strong and you smell so good." Then he took off flying, and as he left he sang this song to the mint plants: "Round and round the Buzzard goes; where he will land next, nobody knows."

Crane or Egret

This bird is the peacemaker and fisherman. He is a good-luck sign while you are fishing, or during conflict. He brings peace, stability, harmony, and good luck. He is graceful, tactful, and direct. The feathers from these birds are used in healing ceremonies to take away negative energy and anger, and to bring peace and harmony to a situation. That is one reason why our Indian people use different kinds of feathers in different kinds of rituals and ceremonies. The symbol and inherent power of the feathers from certain birds are used to bring in specific kinds of spirits and energies. For example, my uncle Lester had to attend a special meeting a few years ago with the U.S. Forest Service representatives concerning joint-land-use plans and proposals. The meeting came about as a result of conflict between different groups all wanting to use USFS land in different ways. Uncle Les did not want to get into any heated arguments with other people at the meeting. So he prayed on a Snowy Egret feather, asked the bird to share its power with him, and he wore it in his hat at the meeting. The meeting became peaceful and cooperative.

Eagle

▼▼▼

Eagles are always very special and good signs. They represent protection, wealth, wisdom, foresight, strength, and spirituality. If one or more should approach while you are praying or performing a ceremony, then you know your prayers have been answered. If I see an Eagle sitting in a tree, on a telephone pole, or alongside the road while I am traveling, I know it is telling me that I will encounter a spiritual person up ahead, such as a medicine man or a ceremonial leader. Or if I am planning on performing a ceremony somewhere and the Eagle comes in, I know that it will be a good group of people and a good ceremony. Sometimes the Great Creator sends in an Eagle just to check up on us, so when we see this, we always give special thanks to the Creator and the Eagle. The Eagle carries our prayers directly to the Great Creator.

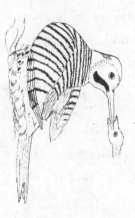

Flickerbird

▼▼▼▼▼▼▼

Flickerbird is a good sign and a good protector. If you hear him whistle, he is trying to tell you that a visitor is coming or company is about to call you on the telephone. It is good luck to have Flickerbirds around the house and yard. They bring happiness, good luck, and healing. They are also messengers for lightning and thunderstorms. If a flock of Flickerbirds suddenly land in your yard or around the house and make a bunch of noise, it is a sign that a thunderstorm is forthcoming.

Goose

▼▼▼▼

Geese bring messages about the seasons, and they tell us when fall is coming or when spring is coming. In this sense they are a good sign. They also serve as reminders that we need to get our life in order, become more organized, and be more cooperative. They teach us the need for supporting one another and the need to assume the role of leadership when the existing leaders become too weak. For example, you can see them start to gather and fly south before winter begins, or hear them return to the north when spring is about to arrive. In such cases stop and study their behavior and you will see how they plan and cooperate in their flight patterns.

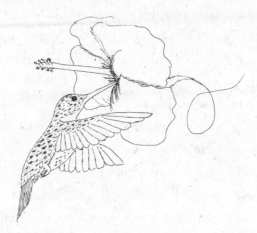

Hummingbird

Hummingbird is a very good sign. She is a good-luck messenger. She takes our prayers to the Great Creator. She is a doctor and healer. The Hummingbird has the power to travel long distances under great odds and obstacles. Her colors promote healing and balance. She is very smart and very spiritual. She can teach us how to soul-travel, develop psychic powers of the mind, and how to be graceful.

Here is a very ancient story that a medicine man and hereditary chief for the Seneca Indians, Beeman Logan, told me when I was a young man. He called it "Hummingbird's Outerspace Trip."

A very long time ago, the animals and birds gathered for a great meeting by Thunder Rocks, which is now located in Allegany State Park, in New York State. This is where they used to meet to discuss important and complicated matters concerning the Earth, powers, religion, and spiritual training. Sometimes they discussed philosophical concerns involving Creation itself.

This one particular time, they all met to discuss the mysterious Creation of the Universe (humans had not been created yet). Bear, who was chief at the time, addressed the council meeting and said: "I wonder if we are the only people in the world."

At first there was dead silence; then suddenly came an uproar of arguments as each person tried to present a viewpoint. Some argued that we were the only people in the world. Others argued that there had to be other people somewhere.

Wolf stood up and growled, very mean, and in so doing got everyone's attention. He was a wise man and leader, and was well respected. He said: "Only a fool would think like that." Then the arguments and uproar continued. Finally, it was Raven who stood up and said: "I believe we should settle this with a contest instead of a fight." So he suggested that someone with special powers be chosen to fly past the Sun and find out if we are indeed the only people in the world.

All creatures were then organized for a great race. Some on the sidelines began to place bets: "I'll wager on Eagle," said Turtle, knowing that there was no way a Turtle could fly. Muskrat said he would bet on Hawk, and Frog said: "I will bet my money on Buzzard because he is the biggest and strongest and can endure any kind of hardship." And so it went until only the Bird people were left in line for the great race, because only they had the power to fly.

One by one they shot off at a very fast speed, flying higher and higher, until only Eagle could be seen, as a small dot in the sky. As he flew higher and higher, he began to look down upon the other birds and brag: "I guess I am the most beautiful bird in the world, so I guess I will have to find out the secret." But soon he too began to weaken. Then he felt something on his head. It was Hummingbird. She had brought her own food for the trip, a tiny mustard seed.

"Thank you, brother, for the lift," she said, and off she hummed, into the darkness, far past the Grandfather Sun. In the meantime, the other people waited and waited and waited for her return. Finally, after seven days, they heard a loud humming noise, and coming from the east was Hummingbird. There was a great commotion of excitement and then the jealous Owl stood up and asked: "Well, what proof do you have of your trip and accomplishment, tiny one. Are we the only people in the world?"

Hummingbird reached into her small pocket and pulled out a small, sparkling quartz crystal and responded: "No, because I traded my mustard seed, my food, for this sacred healing rock with these other people in outer space, who live on other planets in the Universe. Someday they will come to visit us and you will have more proof."

Magpie

The Magpie is a good bird and a good sign. He is a messenger and tells us the road up ahead is clear of danger while we are traveling. He can tell us that company is coming for a visit. Sometimes when we are sad and depressed, he will come to listen to our problem and tell us how to resolve it. The elders say that Magpie is wise, that he knows things; that he is clever and can figure out how to solve problems easily. He is a good talker and listener. He is a real friend to humans, and can provide guidance. He is cunning, crafty, and a survivor, so he can also give us good advice. He represents intelligence. A Blood/Blackfeet friend of mine, the young medicine man Raymond Many Bears, from Standoff, Canada, once told me a story about Magpie and the Buffalo. It goes something like this:

A long time ago, the Buffalo were so big, strong, and fierce that they dominated the world. They could hurt anyone, at any time, and do anything they wanted. In fact, at one time they even ate people.

They were taking over the world, and everyone was afraid of them. This was long before we had horses to hunt with, and when our people lived in small bands and families for survival. It was long before the White people came to this country. It was a time in our history when the Bison ruled the world from one end of the country to the other. Not even the mighty Grizzly Bear, Elk, or Mountain Lion had a chance.

The people became so frightened of the Buffalo, they decided to conduct a four-day ceremony and hold council with the Great Spirit. They brought out their most sacred pipes and most powerful medicine bundles. They sweated, fasted, prayed, and meditated for a vision to seek guidance on how to resolve their problem with the Bison.

The Great Spirit felt sorry for them, so he sent Magpie to listen and help. The Magpie went to the Buffalo and told them that what they were doing was wrong, and that the Great Spirit was angry with them. He told them that they had better behave or there would come a day when they would all disappear from the face of the Earth. The

Buffalo didn't believe Magpie, but he kept pestering them and following them around, until they finally agreed on a way to settle it. They decided to have a great race. If the Buffalo won, they could continue to dominate everyone and eat humans if they so desired. If the other creatures won, then humans could hunt, kill, and eat Buffalo. And in exchange, the Buffalo would give the humans everything they needed to survive.

So the great race got started. All the different creatures in Nature lined up alongside the Buffalo. Coyote hollered to start the race and they all took off, leaving a large cloud of dust that hid everything from sight. One by one the other animals and humans fell by the wayside. The Elk and Deer were fast for a while, but they too began to fall behind the mighty Buffalo.

Magpie saw that the situation was desperate and decided to help. He flew ahead in the cloud and landed on the lead Buffalo's horns. Just before they all got to the finish line, he flew off and was waiting for the arriving herd. He had won the contest for the humans. Ever since, he has told us where to find the Buffalo whenever we had a difficult time in hunting.

Osprey or Fish Hawk

This is a very good bird and power, but a very bad sign. It means you should beware of a potentially dangerous and lethal accident. One time my mother-in-law and her husband were traveling to Eureka, California, from the town of Klamath on the reservation. As they entered within the city limits, they noticed a Fish Hawk swoop down as if trying to snatch the car. They knew it meant something bad, but they didn't know what to do about it. Then the car suddenly went dead at a busy intersection. My mother-in-law's husband, Kenny, decided to get out of the car and look under the hood. Suddenly a Fish Hawk came down and dropped a fish directly on the hood of the car. Kenny had one hand on the hood and, upon seeing the frightening and bizarre incident, jumped back. The battery blew up, almost killing him. He could have had his head blown off if he had not jumped out of way when the Fish Hawk dropped the fish. He did receive minor burns and injuries, but got his wife out of the car before the rest of it caught on fire.

Fish Hawks warn of serious danger on the river, lake, and ocean while one is traveling in a boat. One should always heed their warning and look carefully for possible immediate danger, such as the sudden appearance of a large log, rock, or debris in the boat's path. I know of a situation where I shared this knowledge with some people from Mississippi and Louisiana, and it kept them from falling into a nest of deadly Water Moccasin Snakes while water-skiing. They saw the sign and avoided the area.

Owl

All Owls are a bad sign, but different kinds bring somewhat different messages, and different degrees of power and knowledge. Western people believe in the "wise old owl" image, which is partially correct because the Owl symbolically has this kind of power, but it can be used in a negative way. The Owl is a favorite ally of sorcerers who have clairvoyant powers but use them for selfish desires: for ego, for profit, or to control and manipulate others. The Owl is considered a bad sign and a bad power by most Native American tribal groups. It is a messenger of evil, of sickness, or of a fatal accident. It is also considered a sign of death. Therefore, if you hear or see an Owl hooting around your house, it is considered a bad sign. The closer it is to the house, the closer the relative to be affected. It warns of a potential death that can come in the form of accidents or diseases. The book *I Heard the Owl Call My Name*, by Margaret Craven, and the current movie *Thunderheart* both provide examples of the Owl symbolically serving as a messenger of death.

Here is a short Indian story that can also serve as an example of the Owl's power. It was told to me by Chief Ed Chiloquin from the Klamath Indians in Oregon. He called it "Owl's Warrior Medicine."

Many, many generations ago, sometime in the Beginning, the Great Creator made all the Bird people, as he did most other things in this world. But there was an evil one, the Evil Spirit who tried to imitate the Great Creator. He wanted to show that he had power, too. So he made a bird that was not noisy and noticeable like all the other birds. This one was quiet, deadly quiet. No one could hear it fly. No one saw it during the day, and seldom did anyone hear its voice because it did not sing. And no one ever saw it with other birds.

Anytime the Indian people went on a vision quest, to ask for help from the Great Creator and to quest for a good power and spirit guide, this strange bird would be the first thing to come in. He would say:

"Look at my eyes; see how strange they are, but how much power I have in them. My eyes look like the Sun and I can see anything, here, far away, or even into the future. That is why nothing can hide from me. And I am strong; I can kill anything with my claws. I am a good hunter and warrior; I am silent and can sneak up on anything and kill it without it noticing me. That is what I do, so if you really want power, then take me."

So, a long time ago, an ancient man took that power. If people did not do what he wanted, or if he became jealous or angry, then he sent his Owl power against them. After a while the people became very afraid of this Owl man. But sometimes they would hire him, paying him a lot of money to hurt or kill others they did not like. The Owl man liked his job and reputation. He became quite famous.

The people sent their best warriors against him, but they could not kill the Owl man. They used their best doctors and medicine people to fight off the sickness, disease, accidents, and death being created by him. But they could not stop him. Sometimes he would change shape, into a smaller Owl or a bigger Owl. He could even blend into the color of the trees, the night, or the snow.

One day the people held a sacred sweat-lodge ceremony and prayed. They cried to the Great Creator about their problem with the Owl man, and asked for help. The Creator sent Raven and Coyote to help the people, because they were monster slayers. They went and fought and destroyed the Owl man. And that is what we use even today to protect ourselves from the Owl. Beware if you ever hear an Owl hoot around your house, but don't fear it. Beware if you see an Owl look and holler at you in broad daylight because it is really Death himself that is stalking you. It is a sign you are going to die unless you have the knowledge, power, and ability to stop it.

❖   ❖   ❖

Although most Native American groups have historically considered the Owl a negative sign and bad power, they still respect it, realizing that there are two sides to everything in life. That which is negative can be turned around into a positive situation, if one has the proper kind of knowledge and esoteric training. For example, there have been a number of different occasions in my life when I was driving at night and an Owl flew across the front of the car to warn us of danger. In one situation black ice was on the road, which was difficult to see. Another time a horse was standing in the middle of the road. And there have been numerous times when we couldn't see a narrow bridge covered by fog. The Owls warned us of the potential danger by flying in the direction of the bridge. On another occasion the Owl forewarned us of a bad car accident caused by a drunken driver, which had blocked the roadway. In each situation I heeded the warning, slowing the vehicle down to a very cautious speed and looking carefully for the potential danger. I also took time to thank the Owl for giving me the omen and message, and I sang a prayer song for protection. When such bad signs or omens appear, we are taught to burn a smudge stick made from cedar or sage, and pray to the Great Creator and good spirits for protection. (Some Indian people carry sweet grass braids and/or angelica root in their cars while traveling for this purpose.)

Quail

Quail are good signs. They symbolically communicate that a friendly person is coming. For example, if you are out for a walk on an isolated road or path in the woods and suddenly a Quail appears near you, it is letting you know that a friendly person is going to cross your path. If a covey of Quail show up near your house, it means a family is coming. If one Quail suddenly runs in front of you, dances around in a kind of

crazy manner as if all nervous and excited, but doesn't fly away, then it is telling you that someone up ahead finds you attractive and will probably flirt with you.

Raven and Crow

▼▼▼▼▼▼▼▼▼▼

The Raven and the Crow are always good signs, but they have distinct, often multiple messages and meanings. Both birds are good-luck signs of protection and messengers of wealth. If you see a Raven or a Crow eating or flying with food in its mouth, then it means you are going to get a gift or some money. The power symbols of the Raven and the Crow can be used to counteract or checkmate bad signs and omens, or to fight against bad signs or spirits, such as the Owl. I always watch out for bird signs while traveling. If I see a Hawk, I know she is warning me of danger, so I prepare for the danger and thank the Hawk. But afterward, if I see a Raven or a Crow, I know the road or my path is clear; the danger has gone away.

We have a ceremony in our tribes in northwestern California, where we use the symbol, power, and prayers of the Crow to make warrior medicine and protection. (This special kind of dance, prayer, and ceremony is kept secret.) My father-in-law had the ceremony performed on him when he went into World War II. He was part of the 101st Airborne's Screaming Eagles, during the Normandy invasion. He lived, while others around him were either wounded or killed. I know of Indian friends and relations who used the same medicine, power, and ceremony before going to Vietnam. They came back unharmed. That is how powerful this knowledge and the use of certain birds as spirit allies can be.

In my previous book *Native Healer*, I talk about the sign of the Raven appearing each time I died and came back to life. The Raven is one of the very few natural powers and supernatural aids that can go over into the land of the deceased, into the spirit world, and bring a person's soul back to the physical world, hence bringing that person out of a coma or back to life. (This kind of knowledge is a high shamanistic form of philosophy and symbolism and requires specialized training in mythology and esoterics.)

The Raven and the Crow are also used for hunting medicine and power. We make prayers and recite an ancient prayer about the Raven or the Crow prior to going on a hunt, and the bird will always lead us to game such as a Deer, Elk, Moose, Mountain Goat, whatever. We also always promise to leave some of the food in return for his services!

Here is a story about Crow that I heard from a Yurok Indian elder, Frank Douglas. He called it "Crow's Test."

In the Beginning there were no people, trees, animals, or birds on the Earth yet. There was nothing except spirits. When the proper time had arrived, the Great Creator decided the world must be populated with birds, animals, fish, bugs, humans, and all those who walk, crawl, fly, and swim. He called the spirits together, and there were many, even more than the stars. He told them that the time had arrived when the world must take on its burdens and fulfill its purpose. Each spirit would be permitted to choose what it wanted to be, after the Great Creator had described what their roles and duties would be.

Some wanted to be the different creatures in Nature, and some wanted to be humans. One spirit wanted to be the most beautiful bird in the world: a Crow with a beautiful crest, red shoulders, a large red spot at the base of his tail, and red legs.

The Great Creator said to this spirit: "You will have to stand the test before you can be such a beautiful bird and have such sacred colors. Every spirit must stand a rigid test to prove that it is worthy to take on the life and appearance of that which it chooses to be. You must fly to the ocean with your eyes shut and land in the shallow water that is left after the waves have started to recede. You must then wade up to your knees, or even a bit deeper, and then come back to me without having opened your eyes. I will then judge your worthiness."

Crow flew away to the ocean and waded in up to his knees. He felt something bumping into his legs and became curious. He opened his eyes and looked down and saw small fish trying to eat the short feathers that grew just above his knees. He had been flying for one moon with his eyes shut, and he was very hungry. Crow decided he would eat just one little fish. After all, nobody would really know. Anyway, he tried to rationalize, the Great Creator could not be so unjust as to penalize him for that.

The little fish tasted so good that he ate another, and another, and another, until he was full and too stuffed to even fly. Then Crow heard a rushing noise as if a heavy wind had blown in to shore. Turning around, he beheld the Great Creator watching him.

Crow waded ashore and confessed to the Great Creator, expressing his remorse. The Great Creator however, said: "You have not obeyed me and are not worthy of your request. You will be a Crow, but you cannot have any beautiful red feathers, nor red legs, and all the Crows who come into this world hereafter will forever be black, from their beaks to their claws."

The spirits who desired to be other creatures also had to pass a test in order to earn special powers. These powers can be a gift to mankind if only they know how to use them. And so it was also with the spirits who wanted to be human beings. Some had to show their ability to handle a canoe, others to prove their marksmanship for hunting, some in the talent of making fine baskets, and others in leadership or healing.

Robin

Robin is a good singer. She brings happiness, good health, and love to families. It is good to have Robins around. Remember the old saying "The early bird gets the worm"? We can learn good behavior and values from the Robin, such as being industrious. If you want to learn how to be a good singer, ask Robin to help you. Robin is a proud bird, clean, and well dressed. She is industrious, cheerful, and family-oriented. She is a good reminder of virtues worth emulating and a good role model for humans.

Seagull

The Seagull is a survivor. He can go for long periods of time without food and survive under the worst conditions. He represents stamina, perseverance, and cunning. But he can also be mischievous, selfish, and quarrelsome. If you see a flock of Seagulls inland flying around in circles, it is a warning that a bad storm is coming. The power of the Seagull can also get rid of negative powers, such as when thousands of

grasshoppers ravaged the Midwest back in the 1930s. Seagulls were sent by the Great Creator to purify the pestilence. Seagulls will eat anything if they have to.

Turkey

The Turkey is a good sign, but its character is arrogant, colorful, sneaky, quick-minded, and tricky. Turkeys can warn of people's personality. If you happen to see a Turkey just before a visitor comes, it is an indication that your visitor is nervous, arrogant, fickle in decision-making, and unreliable. However, Turkey feathers are highly respected by some Native tribal groups and are used as part of ceremonial regalia.

A long time ago, all the Bird people gathered for a meeting and celebration to give thanks to the Earth for all the food they had gotten during the fall harvest. This was also a good time for the women (female birds) to check out the men (male birds), to see which one they considered the best-looking, and a possible mate.

A lot of the women kept studying Eagle. Some liked Hawk, while others thought Woodpecker was the best-looking and had the prettiest colors. In the meantime, Turkey was bashful at first and kept hiding in and out of the brush. His friends urged him to come out and visit, but he became too nervous.

Blue Jay hollered and squawked at him. She told the other birds: "He is too slim, plain-looking, and sneaky. No woman in her right mind would want him!" This made Turkey mad. It hurt his feelings to the point where he rushed out in front of everyone and started to squawk back at Blue Jay. All of a sudden his chest raised up and all kinds of beautiful, large feathers encircled him. He now strutted around proud, big, and colorful; and his dancing really impressed the women so much that some of them chased after him. But Turkey was too fast and got away in the thicket.

Woodpecker

▼▼▼▼▼▼▼

Woodpeckers are good signs. They are symbols of wealth, good luck, happiness, and healing. If you hear or see a Woodpecker pecking on a tree near your house, clap your hands three times, make a wish, and thank him for the message and gift. He will usually bring you good luck—a sign that money or a gift is coming. Or if someone is sick in the household, or even dying in the hospital, the woodpecker is a good sign that that person will get healed and well.

Wren and Other Small Birds

Our elders teach us that the Great Creator really loves the little birds, and to each species he gave a special power. The Black-headed Wren we call the Snow Bird. It tells us when it is going to snow and from what direction it will come. The Chickadee lets us know when other people are gossiping about us or talking about us in a bad way. The Swallow tells us when spring is coming and what the other weather elements will be like. And all small-sized birds warn us of bad weather, earthquakes, tornadoes, hurricanes, and even droughts. We are told never to kill these little birds unless we intend to eat them. But most of them are too small to eat or to use in regalia or for artifacts.

They are messengers from the spirit world. Some of our elders say they are actually our ancestors coming to visit. Their songs are good medicine and make people happy. My grandma used to say: "If you suddenly notice that everything is quiet and the birds have stopped their constant chattering and singing, then beware." So we are taught to feed them, and it is lucky to have them around the house.

We are also told that the Great Creator sends the little birds around to check up on us, to evaluate our behavior, and to listen to our prayers. If a bird flies into the house and tries to stay in the house, it is a very bad sign. It means that someone in that family is going to die, unless you can get a medicine man/woman to come and pray for the family and use his/her power to avert the situation.

Here is a story I heard about Wren from my wife Tela's elderly Karuk aunt, Beverly Donahue:

One day Wren and all the other little birds went down the river to fight the Yurok Indians. Just before they got there, they all stopped at Bluff Creek to eat. This was like a dividing line between the territories of the Karuk, Yurok, and Hupa Indians. It was also considered Big Foot's personal fishing place.

Blue Jay volunteered to cook the acorns, while everyone was eating dried Deer meat. One acorn kept bubbling up in the pot. Buzzard, being a curious fellow, kept watching the acorn and assumed it was the only one in the pot. So every time Blue Jay turned her back he would try to snatch it up and eat it, but the soup was too hot for him. That is how he got a burned and bald head.

Soon the acorns were cooked. Blue Jay drained the hot water off, and as it ran down the hillside, lots of acorns rolled out. This, of course, caught the attention of the Mice, Chipmunks and Woodpeckers. They began to fight over the acorns.

Hawk was concerned about the fighting, so he asked Wren to sing him a song. Then Wren said, "My song is not that good, so I'd better not. I don't think it will cause them to stop fighting."

"Oh, that is all right," said Hawk. "Give it a try anyway."

But the Wren argued back, "My song is too powerful, and it could cause a great storm. No, I don't think I should sing it." Hawk insisted and became somewhat threatening. So Wren sang. At the first note a big windstorm came up, and the first big puff of wind blew Hawk back up the river. That is how strong it was.

"See, I told you my song was bad," said Wren. "That is all right," hollered Hawk. "Just keep singing." Eventually he was blown all the way up the river back to his home, which is what he really wanted all along anyway. That way he didn't have to go to war and worry about getting hurt.

* * *

Here is another story about Wren, Eagle, and Grouse you might find interesting. Try to figure out the symbolic meaning and message in this story!

Once, in the olden days, Eagle was going along and he met Wren. Wren had a small bow and arrows and Eagle began to laugh at them.

"What are you doing? You can't shoot anything with those, brother; they're too small."

"I can shoot very far with these," answered the Wren. "Why don't you go out to that ridge over there and I'll prove it. I will shoot at you."

Eagle looked out to the right and laughed some more. "There is no way you can shoot that far," he said. "I can't even shoot that far." And he stood there laughing and putting down the Wren.

After a while he was walking on the ridge looking for mice when Raven came along. Eagle was happy to see his cousin and he forgot about Wren. Then suddenly he heard a strange sound and looked around to see what it was. Wren's arrow had hit him right in the heart. In shock, he jumped over and fell dead. But Raven, who has a special power, pulled out the arrow and jumped over Eagle four times; he sang a song that sounded like whistling, and brought Eagle back to life.

"I must have slept for a long time," Eagle said as he got up.

"You weren't sleeping, you were dead as a log. Wren's arrow struck you in the heart. So why did you tease him? After all, you know he can shoot better than anyone," said Raven. This made Eagle embarrassed and angry. "I will get even with him," he said.

Some time afterward Eagle found Wren and proposed a gambling contest. "I have your arrow here. Now you can get it back, if you play this game of arrows with me." They competed against each other, but Eagle won every time. In fact, Eagle won everything from Wren, including his beautiful set of feathers.

But Wren had a plan. He began to follow Eagle. Eventually Eagle came to the lodge of Grouse, who had ten young children. The parents were off looking for food. Eagle asked them: "Who is your father?"

One of them responded, "Flying-past-your-head."

"No," said Eagle. "That cannot be a real name." Then he asked again, "Then who is your mother?"

"Flying-past-your-legs," said another Grouse child. Eagle went into their house and dug a small hole near the fire. Then he said to one of the Grouse children, "Put some red bearberries into this hole and watch me cook them for you." The children did as they were told and then crowded around Eagle, watching. Suddenly he grabbed them all and pushed them into the hole. Then he covered them up with dirt and hot ashes. When they were cooked, he went on his way.

Afterward the parents came home and found their Grouse children dead, and they began to cry. Wren heard the noise and asked why they were crying. They told him what Eagle had done.

"I have a grudge against Eagle, too," he said. "I want my things back from him. So if you help me get them back, I will use my power and restore your children back to life."

The Grouse parents agreed and flew after Eagle.

Eagle was found going up a mountain trail. The two Grouse made a detour and came around in front of him. When Eagle tried to catch them, they just flew at his head. Eagle tried to reach the edge of the cliff to get away from their attack. Then the other Grouse flew between Eagle's legs so fast that it caused him to lose his balance. He fell off the cliff. The Grouse hurried and plucked him as he was falling down.

They got the bow and arrows and Wren's clothing and gave them back to Wren. This made Wren very happy. So he sang his song over the Grouse children and brought them all back to life. Once again Raven came around looking for his cousin and found him dead. Since

he wanted a hunting companion, he jumped over Eagle four times, squawked loudly, and brought him back to life. Ever since this time, you won't see those birds hanging around together because they are all mad at Eagle.

Insect Signs and Omens

Ant
▼▼▼

Ant represents super strength, intelligence, psychic abilities, telepathic communication, sharp thinking, and planning. The big Black Ant warns of earthquakes. Red biting Ants are bad powers and challengers. Other kinds of Ants can be messengers and allies. Small Ants are a nuisance.

A number of years ago, my wife and I were asked to do a presentation in San Francisco, California. The sponsor of the workshop and his friends treated us to lunch at an expensive restaurant downtown. We sat around the table talking about Native American religion, ritual symbolism, and spirituality. Our conversation was suddenly interrupted by the unusual appearance of a large Black Ant slowly walking across a pure white tablecloth. It was as if some unknown power was making us all aware of his presence. The attention of everyone at the

table was focused on this Ant, and there was dead silence around the table. He stopped directly in front of me, then danced around in a circle four times, made two small jumps, and headed south over the edge of the table and out of sight. One of our visitors reacted: "I can't believe it! I know there is some kind of communication going on here, but I don't know what. After all, one rarely sees any kind of bug in a clean and expensive restaurant. This large Ant just appears out of nowhere, as if by magic, at exactly the same time we are talking about omens. He marches across the table straight to you. And you talk to him in your Native language while he does a little dance, and after you tell him thank you, he disappears! What is all this about? Does it mean something?"

I tried to tell my friend that it was not a coincidence. It was a sign, an omen, and an example of "synchronicity," as the famous psychologist Carl Jung called it (meaning that such things are not coincidental). The Ant is a sign and messenger from Nature, and it was telling us that a very big earthquake was coming and would be here within four days, preceded by two small warning quakes, with the large one occurring south of San Francisco. Some of the people at our table laughed and said: "Well, we have earthquakes here a lot, so what?"

My wife and I canceled our sightseeing plan and a series of job interviews that had been scheduled for me over the next few days. Because we understood the symbolic omen, we went back to Spokane, Washington. Exactly four days after we left, a very bad earthquake hit Hayward. Bridges were knocked down, buildings demolished, people seriously injured and killed. Roads in the San Francisco Bay Area were blocked off due to damage and chaos from the natural catastrophe. It was one of the worst earthquakes in Northern California in recent times.

There is an old Wiyot Native myth that teaches us about Earthquake and Ant. I learned it from a Wiyot Indian elder named Albert James. It goes something like this:

A long time ago, Earthquake and his brothers were giants. They lived underground because the Lightning and Thunder giants ruled the sky. Earthquake and his brothers were mischievous bullies who went around pestering everyone. From tiny bogs to large trees, from the valley to the mountains—everywhere they went they left behind a mess.

The Native people who lived along the Pacific Coast built solid, sturdy houses made from the large redwood trees. They figured such houses could stand up against anything. But Earthquake and his brothers would run by and try to knock the houses into the ocean. After a while the people got angry and decided to do something about it. They fasted for five days in the sacred sweat lodge and prayed. They cried out to the Great Spirit for help and protection.

One day a large Black Ant came into the sweat lodge and crawled up on the village headman. He said: "I can help you. I am very, very strong. I will challenge Earthquake and his brothers to a shinny stick game. Whoever wins will get a special wish."

The Native people just laughed. "How can such a little fellow like you beat a giant?" they asked. "Because I have a special power, and you will see it," replied the Ant. "Do you want my help or not?"

Well, the Native people were so scared and so desperate that they were willing to try anything. Arrangements were made to play the shinny game, a rough sport somewhat like field hockey. At daybreak the two teams came out on the grassland. Instructions were given, bets were made, and agreements were made about winning. Earthquake promised that if they lost, they would always send out a messenger to the Native people before going on a run or rampage. However, it was also agreed that if Earthquake won, they would go wherever they wanted to go, do whatever they wanted to do, and have all the fun they wanted without having to worry about reprimands from the Great Creator. The Ants played a tough game against Earthquake. They ran, tossed, fought, and struggled all day from sunrise until sunset. They beat Earthquake and his brothers into submission. That is how Black Ant became man's friend and messenger. And that is also why the Native people do not build their houses upon Ants' nests.

Bee

▼▼▼

A Bee is a messenger with news about sex. If you see a Bee fly close by or in your house, then you know what is on the person's mind who came to visit. Bees can be used for fertility, protection, and love power. Yellow Jackets, Hornets, Wasps, and similar types of bugs are bad signs and signal that a challenge or nuisance is up ahead. For example, I was at a female friend's house visiting and trying to provide her with spiritual counseling. A Yellow Jacket flew into the house and tried to sting or bite me. I told her it was a sign that somebody was coming who didn't like me, and they would act mean toward me. As it turned out, a male friend of hers came over and kept trying to provoke an argument. It was obvious he was jealous and overprotective.

Beetle
▼▼▼▼

Some Beetles are good signs, and some are bad signs and bad powers. You need to learn which ones mean what in your area by studying their behavior and what occurs after you see one. Some Beetles are messengers of good or bad weather or environmental changes. Rolling Thunder used the power of the Beetle to bring lightning and thunder and rain, and to change the weather when necessary. In some cases beetles have devastated acres of trees, but they symbolically warned everyone before the attack.

A couple of years ago, my publisher from Quest Books decided to fly me to New York to attend a national publishers' and authors' convention. One of the senior staff leaders from Quest, John White, who has since become a close friend of mine, offered to be my guide, which I gladly accepted. I was staying in an old but well-known hotel across from Madison Square Garden. The national conference, which would include thousands of people from around the world, was to be held in the gigantic convention center. Quite frankly, I was anxious, nervous, and somewhat afraid of New York City. There were just too many people there. It was too crowded and too crazy for me. I was not impressed at all, but decided to participate for public relations reasons and to promote my new book, *Native Healer*. Anyway, John and I were down in the hotel lobby and I had just smudged myself with "Grizzly Bear Root" (angelica herb) for protection as part of a ritual I use for dealing with stress and anxious situations. I went down to the lobby to look for John. He caught me talking to a large Beetle-type bug that I

had suddenly seen run in from nowhere and snatch a smaller bug that was near the front door of the lobby. I think he was embarrassed by my behavior and reacted accordingly, but I could tell that he was also curious. So I told him what I had just seen. I told him that it was an omen, a messenger from Nature. I also told him that I felt uneasy about the place and its location, and I didn't really care to venture out to go sightseeing. I felt something bad was about to happen. I told John that the bug scenario was a warning that someone we knew might get robbed or hurt. Well, as things turned out, the editor of our company was just getting out of a taxi at the front door of the hotel when all of a sudden a man ran up, pushed her back into the taxi, snatched her purse, and fled down the street, all within a few minutes. She lost everything but luckily didn't get hurt.

Butterfly

The Butterfly is a very spiritual bug and represents the presence of good spirits. Butterflies signal change, metamorphosis, balance, harmony, grace, peace, beauty, and spirituality. They are a good sign. Not long ago, my oldest daughter was in her bedroom trying to meditate and focus on her Moontime (menses) ritual. It was wintertime, when it is very rare to see a Butterfly. She started hollering excitedly for my wife Tela and me to come and look at the beautiful Butterfly in her bedroom. She wanted to know how it got there, especially during such a cold winter. The colors had special, symbolic meaning for my daughter. So we both told her it was a special ancestor spirit who had come to check up on her, and to communicate with her while she was using her menses as a spiritual time. That night my daughter woke me up from my sleep. I could hear her laughing and talking very loud. So I got up to check on her. She was sitting on the side of the bed, in a dream state, pointing to the Butterfly and calling it "Grandmother." "Look, Daddy, can you see her? She is very big now. She is opening her wings and telling me to come over for a hug, but she keeps changing from a pretty young girl into an old and wise woman. She wants me to feed her and come fly with her. Should I go, Daddy? I am scared; can I trust her?" I couldn't wake my wife up from her deep sleep to handle this situation, which is considered "women's matters," so I told my daughter to offer the Butterfly spirit some flowers and oatmeal cookies and go over and give her a hug. I told my daughter not to be afraid, that it was a good spirit and a good sign. I told her to be brave and fly with the "Grandmother." The next morning my daughter told us all of her fortunate and beautiful dreams about the Butterfly. She was convinced it was all just a dream, until the Butterfly came flying from her bedroom and out the front door.

Cockroach

This bug is considered a bad bug and a bad sign. It warns that sickness, disease, or even undesirable and unpleasant people will be coming to your home. It is dirty and bothersome yet a tenacious survivor. Sorcerers work with bad bugs like this and can send whole swarms of them against another person.

I once saw a Cockroach try to climb on my pants just before I went to meet with a small group of people who, on the surface, appeared to be genuinely interested in spiritual assistance. But when I got to the meeting I noticed one person in particular who seemed sneaky in character. During the meeting this person became very rude and bothersome, at other times downright crude. It didn't take me long to realize that she was on drugs and was hoping to get some Indian medicine from me "that might give a person a real high."

In another situation I was staying in a motel in the Southwest. Just before I came out of my room, a bunch of Cockroaches ran in front of me and tried to get into my room. I talked to them and told them I was sorry to hurt them, but under the Creator's laws I had the right to defend myself. So I tried to gather them up and take them outside, to get them away from me. Later that night, while walking back to my room, I was harassed by a small group of drunken and unclean-looking characters who wanted to come into my room and party. They got fairly aggressive for a while until I threatened to call the police. Shortly afterward the manager came, upon hearing a disturbance, and had them removed. Cockroaches can show you when to be careful about who you party with or who you invite into your room or life!

Cricket

Cricket is a very bad power, especially in a geographical area where they are not that common and abundant. The presence of a Cricket means that bad prayers or bad wishes are being made against you. As a result, we typically try to catch it, burn it with cedar outside the house, and pray against it. We therefore consider a Cricket a bad sign, a challenger who is trying to bring us harm. In parts of the country, such as South Dakota, where Crickets are abundant, it may not mean the same thing. Some Native people think Cricket is a good singer and a good sign. So when in doubt, look up the local myths and legends for clarification.

Fly and Blowfly
▼▼▼▼▼▼▼▼▼▼

Flies are bad signs. They don't belong in the house, tepee, lodge, or camp. They are messengers of jealousy, can warn of foul weather forthcoming, and they bring sickness and disease. They are considered a pestilence. The large Blowflies, the kind that feed on defecation, carcasses, and trash are always bad signs. They represent evil and dark forces. The more Flies that show up around you, the worse the situation. It is always best to try to get them out of the house, and if necessary, destroy them in order to protect yourself, your family, and your home. Use cedar or sage to smudge the house and rid it of flies, and call upon the good powers for protection. (See page 172 for more information about this ritual.) Sorcerers and evil people who use the bad powers work with Blowflies as allies. For example, light and burn a smudge stick, and offer it to the Great Creator and the good spirits of the Earth. Open a window or door to your apartment or house. Ask the Great Creator and good spirits to remove all bad bugs and all evil spirits and to protect your life and home. Walk through the entire house while smudging every room. This kind of ritual acts as a spiritual disinfectant.

Grasshopper
▼▼▼▼▼▼▼▼

Grasshopper can warn us of droughts and problems with the weather. For example, too many Grasshoppers in one area means a drought is coming, and hot, dry weather.

I once heard a story about Grasshopper that was told by an elder, Raymond Lagu, from the Pit River tribe in northwestern California:

Grasshopper lived with people who were busy catching salmon and curing it all the time. They said to him one day: "Come and help us. We can prepare for a bad winter this way." But Grasshopper didn't care; he just jumped from place to place, playing and having a good time.

The Ants, who are very intelligent about things, tried again to encourage Grasshopper to be more industrious. "We must prepare now because it is salmon season and the fish are running good," they said while busy at work.

Grasshopper just looked at them and laughed. "No," he said, "I don't like to work. Why don't you come and play with me and have some fun for a while and go around and pester other people?" As he started to leave, he added, "Besides, I don't like fish."

It wasn't long after that that winter came and the abundant grass was all gone. The land was covered in every direction with snow. Grasshopper couldn't have much fun in the snow. It was cold, and he had a hard time finding food. After several days of searching for food, he began to starve. He decided to go begging to the older people. He even begged the Ants for dried salmon.

But nobody would help him. They scolded him and told him to go out and play like he usually does. They teased and pestered him, as he had done to others all summer long.

Finally, when he was barely able to walk and half frozen and starving to death, they felt sorry for him and gave him some food. They said: "Perhaps we need people like Grasshopper as a reminder of what not to be like." And so it has been ever since.

Moth

▼▼▼▼

Moths are messengers from the spirit world, telling us that a ghost is around. I realize that moths are attracted by light and fire, but once again one must study the behavior of the moth to determine if it has gone out of its way and normal pattern to communicate a message. For example, if it lands on your shoulder, ear, or head and keeps following you, it is a messenger from a ghost. A good ghost will give you a warm feeling; a bad ghost will feel cold and eerie, and perhaps pester you. To get rid of it, use the smudge purification ritual and ask the good spirits to take it away.

Spider

▼▼▼▼

Spiders of all kinds are messengers. They can be good signs or bad signs. Usually the poisonous spiders, such as the Wolf Spider, Black Widow, or Tarantula, are bad signs and bad power. The Spider can warn us of small danger. She can tell us that people are jealous, or when a person is lying to us. She can warn us of minor upset or danger. She can tell us about the weather, and she can help us find things. A good Spider does not bite us. A challenger-type messenger does. Sorcerers use Spiders to hurt people and to spy on people. Artists use Spiders to learn how to develop better crafts skills, such as weaving. It is always best not to kill a Spider but to set it outside if it is in the house. Too many spiders in the house is an indication of jealousy, potential conflict, confusion, and bad health forthcoming. When in doubt, study the Spider's behavior. If it acts aggressively, then be forewarned.

A few decades ago, when I was a young boy, my grandmother asked me to go out on the large farm and into the woods to find my cousins and bring them home for lunch. I didn't know in which direction they had gone, so I asked her if she knew. She said, "No, that is why I want you to go find them."

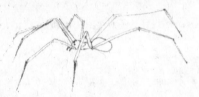

Well, I could have been looking for hours. Realizing the problem ahead, I went to her again and asked: "How will I know where to find them?" She took me over to the side of the house and pointed to a Granddaddy Longlegs Spider. She said, "Ask him, and whatever direction he lifts his legs, that is the direction you should go and search."

Although I felt stupid talking to a Spider, I tried it. The Spider's leg lifted several times to the north. That is the way I went, and I found my cousins. A couple of days later I tried the experiment again. This time the Spider pointed to the south, toward the creek. I still had a hard time believing it, so I went north toward the woods and meadow. My cousins weren't there. Feeling like a fool, I had to turn back south and find them!

Tick

▼▼▼▼▼

Ticks are bad powers and parasites. If you see a lot of ticks early in spring, it is an indication that droughts, diseases, and a lot of forest fires are forthcoming. The presence of ticks in the house is a bad sign and a warning to you to keep your home and family clean and be on guard for disease. If you get bitten by a tick, be sure to twist it out slowly and make sure it is completely removed from the skin. Boil up a small handful of yarrow herb or wormwood (fifteen to twenty minutes), then pack the hot herbal leaves on the bite for about ten minutes, like a poultice to draw out the poison, and drink two cupfuls of the tea a day. Then give the used herbs back to Nature in your yard. This healing approach just might save you from getting Lyme disease!

Reptile and Snake Signs and Omens

Alligator

An Alligator is a challenger. It warns of danger. It can be sent against you by a person of knowledge and power. If you happen to see one, study its behavior well and beware. Become defensive and alert to possible attack by someone or something. The Alligator is considered a bad power.

Frog

Frogs are good signs. The Frog is a doctor and healer, seer, and fortune-teller. The Frog is a messenger of rain, and the power of the Frog can bring rain and water if one knows how to use its power.

On the other hand, Toads are bad power and bad luck. Sorcerers use the power and symbol of the Toad to make bad prayers against people, to cause them sickness, accidents, or harm in some way. If you see Toad, then pray for protection.

Here is an old Indian story I heard called "Frog and the Fire," as told to me by a Karuk elder and famous basket maker, Mrs. Madeline Davis:

A very long time ago, we did not have fire for our sacred dances or to cook with. There was only one tree in the world that had fire in it. This tree didn't want anyone to bother him. He was stingy. He wanted to be the only Fire spirit.

But the birds and animals felt sorry for the Indians. So they held a council meeting. It was agreed there should be more than just one fire in the world.

Coyote said, "I will help get some fire from that tree." And he went to visit the Fire spirit. While he was there, he stole a live coal by putting it between his toes and ran out with it. It was so hot he couldn't carry it all the way by himself. One by one the other animals joined in to help him run the relay. Frog was last, but she was scared. She jumped into the water and hid under some willow roots with it. Ever since that time, the Indians have rubbed the dry willow sticks to help to make fire, and Frog has had skin that looks like it has been burned.

Garden or Garter Snake
▼▼▼▼▼▼▼▼▼▼▼▼▼▼

Garden or Garter Snakes, with different-colored stripes such as yellow, green, or red, are messengers of jealousy. If you see one or several near you, beware of the next person you see or talk to. That person or group of people may be negative, antagonistic, or dishonest.

A number of years ago, I hired one of my neighbor's teenagers to cut the lawn. I paid him ahead of time and then saw him at the mall when he should have been cutting the grass. I was standing outside the mall entrance waiting for my wife when I noticed the teenager trying to duck out of my sight. I called him over and he reluctantly came. I asked him if he had cut the grass, and he said "Yes" and tried to walk away.

But I told him, "You are not telling the truth. The grass has not been cut, and you probably already spent the money." His face turned red with embarrassment, and his smart-mouthed friend responded curtly: "How the hell do you know? Are you psychic or something?"

I simply pointed to a Garden Snake in the grass which was slowly making its way between us, and said: "There is my psychic messenger and proof. You can lie to humans but you can't lie to the spirits. So what is the truth?" The teenager acted both surprised and scared, and admitted to not having done the job. But it did get done later that day!

No snake of any kind belongs in the house, unless it is a pet in a glass container. Anytime a snake comes into the home, it is either a special sign, a messenger, or a challenger. Don't overreact and kill it! You have the right to protect yourself, pray against it, and put it back outside where it belongs. If it is a good snake, thank it for coming to visit you and tell it verbally and spiritually how much you appreciate its visit and assistance. If it is a bad snake, warn it not to come back again and ask it to remove all its malicious intentions as it is leaving. I always address the challenger like this: "My relations in Nature, I am glad that you came to visit me and I know you are coming with bad thoughts. I realize you have special power, but you are violating the Great Creator's law, so I am asking you to leave, and take all your poison and bad medicine back with you. Go back to where you came from and don't return or the Great Creator will punish you." Usually this works, especially if I pray while smudging with cedar or sage (see p. 172) and hold a large bird feather in my hand.

At this point I would like to tell you an old myth about Long Snake, an ancient Karuk Indian story about a man who had a pet snake, as it was told to me by the Karuk ceremonial leader Shan Davis, who died in 1988.

Back in the old days, before the White people came to our country, there was a man who had an interesting experience with a snake. One day it was very hot, so he thought he would go swimming in the Klamath River here, down by Perch Creek. After a while he got tired and decided to swim up to the sandy bank and rest. His foot hit something. At first he thought it was a rock, but upon further investigation he discovered it was a very large egg.

Now, he had heard through old stories that finding such an egg was good luck. That kind of special egg belonged to Long Snake. So he felt fortunate but a little scared. He looked around to make sure nobody saw him, and then he carried it home as fast as he could run. He hid it in his regalia chest, an old handmade cedar chest where a man puts all his religious regalia and medicine.

Every once in a while he would open the chest, check on the large egg, and pray and wish for good luck. His wishes started coming true. He became very lucky at the hand games, gambling, hunting, everything.

Then one morning he went to check on the egg and it had hatched. There he found a baby snake and decided to make it a pet. It also became his power. He always used it when making gambling medi-

147

cine, and he never lost, always winning a lot of dentalia (Indian money) and other kinds of wealth.

He became so famous and wealthy that he bought a wife from a family that was very important in the village. Of course, this meant he had to trade a lot of wealth and regalia for his wife to demonstrate to the other people that she was a very worthy and high-status woman.

As time went on, the snake got bigger. It got too big and long for the cedar chest, and it began to consume more and more food. Although his wife was concerned and started getting a little scared, they would feed it salmon, different kinds of birds, and eventually deer meat.

In time his wife had a baby, and after the ten-day ceremonial restriction she brought it back to the house. The Long Snake became so big, and ate so much, it began to be a threat. It was eating up the family's food supply and it went all over the house doing whatever it wanted to do, becoming a nuisance. It caused concern and arguments in the house, but the lucky man always defended his power and special pet, giving credit for their wealth to this snake.

One day the woman went down to the creek for some water. Her husband was in the sweat lodge purifying himself and praying. She had put the baby in a baby basket, and thought she had secured it up against the wall, near the fireplace. While down at the creek, she heard strange noises coming from the house, and hurried back with the water. She glanced over the side of the trail and saw the Long Snake going down the slope, and sticking out of its mouth she could see the top of the basket and the baby's head. She chased after it, hollering to her husband for help, but the Long Snake crawled down to the river and jumped in, making a big noise and splash. That was the last she ever saw of the Long Snake and her baby.

Lizard

▼▼▼

Most Lizards are harmless but serve as omens. They can talk to you in dreams and bring you messages, be sent against you to spy on you and let someone else know what you are saying or doing, or warn you about weather changes. Small Lizards protect children and babies. They warn adults if the baby is sick or in danger. So the elders say that if you see a Lizard in the house near the baby, don't kill it. It's there to protect the baby from snakes, spiders, bugs, animals, and sickness, and even from bad spirits that may try to steal the baby's soul.

The blue-tailed "Money Lizard" is good luck, a sign that money or a gift is coming. The Gila Monster Lizard is a good protector, and Chameleons are messengers that try to forewarn of a possible sudden change in someone's health, or even in one's lifestyle or home.

Let me tell you a short story about the Lizard, as it was told to me by a Karuk elder named Lottie Beck:

It was Lizard and Coyote who helped make the first babies in the world. They were talking and meditating in the sacred sweat lodge, thinking like they usually do, and this time they were discussing the problem humans had in giving birth to babies.

Lizard said, "Perhaps they should cut a woman open with this white quartz flint to help make the childbirth a little less painful and difficult." Coyote said no, because he thought it would be too dangerous. "Suppose the woman should die," he said. "Then the man would lose a good woman, plus all the regalia he paid for her."

So they prayed, meditated, and thought some more in the sweat lodge. "Then let the baby come out from behind, instead of her mouth," said Lizard, "and this way I will try to help her."

Coyote responded: "Yeah, that's a better idea, but let's make sure that the first baby is a female, because we need more good women in the world."

"OK," said Lizard, "but I am going to help make the boy's hands, feet, and penis while it is still in the woman's stomach. And since he will then look like me, I will always make sure he is protected and grows up to be a warrior."

"OK, OK," hollered Coyote. "If you are going to help the children, then I will help the woman. I will put this medicine in the sweat lodge so the woman in childbirth can chew it and have easy labor while her husband prays and sweats for her in the sweat lodge."

Now ever since, the people instruct boys that they must never kill a Lizard or their skin might get spotted like a Lizard's and bring the people bad luck. And they also say that if a baby laughs when nobody can be seen, it is because Lizard is tickling and playing with the baby. They also say that if the baby is sick and crying, Lizard, who lives around the sacred sweat lodge, will come running and bring his medicine to help the baby. That is why Lizard has good medicine and power. He comes from the sweat lodge, and he fasts a lot and rarely drinks water, which is also why he has power. Although sometimes you can see him hunting around the rocks, he really prefers lying around on top of the sweat lodge.

This ancient myth may seem a little confusing to modern educated and Western thinkers because it has been translated from the Karuk Indian language into English. There are certain symbols and forms of knowledge in the myth that tell the Indian people what kind of powers and spirit allies they can call upon from Nature to use in childbirth and for protection of mothers in labor, and for children. In the old way of childbirth, for example, some women would chew Coyote's medicine and/or drink a tea made from wild ginger and/or pennyroyal herb. They would then ask Coyote to help them have an easy delivery. The woman squatted, sometimes got on her hands and knees, and delivered the baby from behind, instead of lying on her back, as is done in modern times. The umbilical cord was cut with a piece of a white quartz flint type of rock instead of a steel knife. The quartz was thought to be safer, sharper, and less contaminated than steel tools; hence a lesson in health and medicine-making approaches.

Also, boys are taught that Lizards are good protectors. The symbol, power, and song from the Lizard is used in our Karuk Indian War Dance. In order to use this medicine (knowledge and power), a person must fast, abstain from water for a few days, sweat in the lodge, pray, and call upon the spirit of the Lizard as a protector.

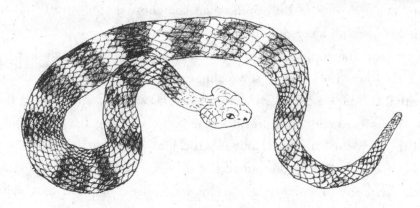

Snake

There are many different kinds of snakes, but I will only concern myself here with species in the United States. Snakes can be wonderful friends because they are very psychic, or what some would call telepathic. They are good hunters and fighters. They have been in existence since the beginning of time, when the world was first created. Like anything else in Nature, they can have good power, bad power, or both. The King Snake is the most powerful in terms of spiritual ranking. He is a good power, a doctor power, used for seeing, healing, and protection. His colors and natural symbols are significant, representing his special knowledge. To have a King Snake living close by your home is a sign of good luck and protection. To see one is a good sign, especially if someone is sick and you have been praying for his or her recovery.

I would like to share a personal experience here as an example of how snakes communicate and use their different powers. Back in 1980 my wife and I were living in a small cabin in the country near the ocean cliffs in Humboldt, California. Our first child, a daughter, was approximately eighteen months old and just learning to walk at the time. One day I got an emergency phone call at work. My wife was upset and in a panic because a large Bull Snake had somehow gotten into the house and was chasing after our toddler daughter. My wife was terrified of snakes, and she couldn't seem to think straight. I tried to talk her into calming down. I told her to stay calm, to approach the situation using a spiritual strategy. I told her to get either a Hawk or Eagle feather, then burn her sacred root and offer it to the Great Creator, the good spirits, and the power of the bird, and ask the Hawk or the Eagle to use its power to chase the Snake out of the house. The first time, she didn't have a chance to go through a ritual because the large Snake had started wrapping itself around our little girl; she reacted on instinct! She grabbed and started beating the Snake off until she had actually swept it back outside. But somehow the Snake managed to get under the front door and come back in. It headed directly for our daughter. So the second time, she grabbed our toddler, put her in the crib, then grabbed the sacred root and the feather, and performed a protection ceremony. She used the Hawk wing to chase the Snake back outside, and then placed a blanket at the base of the door to cover the space. (Hawks love to eat snakes, so it was a wise choice in terms of counteracting powers.) In the meantime, I went outside my office at the college and prayed for my daughter, wife, and home. Using a pipe and tobacco, I asked the Great Creator, the good spirits, and our ancestors to send protection for my family and to put a stop to the sorcery-like harassment. This was a very strange occurrence and it was not simply a coincidence, especially considering the determination of the Bull Snake.

Approximately ten minutes later my wife called again. She said: "Somebody is making a bunch of noise in the front like wrestling or thrashing around." I told her to go outside and see what it was, but she refused. I told her to look out the front window, but her fear and apprehension were so great that again she refused. So I then told her: "Well, go out the back door, around the side of the house, and peer around the corner and see what it is; then call me right back!" A few minutes later she called back and said she saw a very strange and frightening thing. She saw a large Snake with thick white rings coiled around the large Bull Snake. The two were in a desperate fight, thrashing around violently. But in a short time the snake with rings was eating and swallowing the other Snake. I told her that was great! She said, "What do you mean, great? Now what am I supposed to do about the other Snake?"

I replied firmly, "I went out and prayed and asked the Great Creator and the good spirits to send in a patroller for protection, so they sent the King Snake. The one with the black and white or yellow color rings is a King Snake, so just leave him alone and let him do his job. Everything will be just fine now, but don't forget to smudge up the house with cedar and continue praying for protection."

The Bull Snake is usually used as a "power" by Indian gamblers, but sometimes it can be used as an ally against other people, if that happens to be a person's medicine. But the King Snake can only be used in a good way. If you try to plead with him to do otherwise, he will punish you.

The Cottonmouth or Water Moccasin is a bad power. It is poisonous physically and spiritually. Blue or Black Racer is a good power, and is often used to counteract the Cottonmouth or Rattlesnake. The Rattlesnake can be used for good or bad power. The Rattlesnake that is predominantly black in color is a bad power. The White Rattlesnake is a good power. The Timber Rattler is a good power. He is a hunter, warrior, and protector.

The Copperhead Snake can go either way in terms of power. It can be used for fur hunting and protection, or if you have the knowledge can be sent against a person in a bad way. It has a strong power of sight. Its spiritual power can help you develop clairvoyant skills if you learn how to make a psychic connection with it via dreams, visions, or through friendly contacts in Nature.

The Coral Snake is a bad power. In fact, most snakes that are poisonous are considered bad powers, except for such types as the rare albino Rattlesnake and the Timber Rattler. If you see a Coral Snake near your house, on or near your path, don't kill it but pray against it and chase it away. It is a bad sign or omen, a warning that you are going to be challenged by a person with negative thoughts or a jealous attitude toward you. Poisonous snake signs usually mean an enemy is up ahead.

For example, one time I was getting ready to lecture. I was outside smoking and preparing, rehearsing my thoughts. Suddenly I "felt" a snake; I did not see it at first. So I grabbed the medicine pouch around my neck, pulled out some sacred root, and prayed for myself. I asked the Great Creator and the good spirits to "show me the Snake, to let me see the challenger" so I could confront it. A Hawk screamed overhead, circled four times, and began to move in closer to me. While I was studying its movements and praying to it, it suddenly swooped down directly behind me and snatched something from the deep grass. It had a Copperhead in its talons and took it far away.

So I stood on guard and scrutinized the audience carefully. Then I spotted the challenger. It was a man who had come to the lecture to hear what I had to say, and to challenge me culturally and spiritually. To give an analogy, sometimes people in the martial arts do this to each other. This man had power and he wanted to test it out on me, but I didn't go for the challenge. I don't like to lower myself spiritually, to play foolish games with power. He did have knowledge and I could see it in him, in a psychic way, but his power was negative. He was one of those people who study and try to practice sorcery. But for some reason he didn't stay at the lecture long and left quite abruptly, as if he had been snatched from the audience in a mysterious way. So as you can see from this example, we can learn how to interpret bad signs and symbolic communication and then use good symbols and power from Nature to try to protect ourselves.

Turtle

▼▼▼▼

Turtles of all kinds, both water and land Turtles, are good signs and very good powers. The Turtle is considered very sacred to most Native American tribal cultures. The Turtle is a healer and protector. It can grant long life, wisdom, and good health. Our elders tell us never to eat Turtle because doing so can bring bad luck and sickness. Turtle shells are made into dance regalia, and some whole Turtles sacrifice themselves to be used as a power rattle in healing. If a Turtle comes at a time when someone is sick, then it usually is assured that the person will get well and live a long time. But you must make good prayers and wishes to the Turtle at that time in order for the luck to have a better chance of happening. Otherwise it just might take longer to happen. My friend and older mentor Martin High Bear, a Lakota medicine man, told me this story called "A Turtle Who Went to War":

There is an old story among our Lakota people that tells how a long, long time ago the Turtles decided to go on the warpath against the people. The Indians had been greedy and killed more Turtles than they could eat whenever they got lazy and tired of hunting. This made the Turtle chief very angry.

There was a large camp of water Turtles who basically were happy people and minded their own business. But one day they had a special council meeting. They smoked the pipe with the Grasshoppers, Crickets, Butterflies, and even Frogs, Snakes, Fish, and Rabbits. "There are many Indians camped nearby," the women complained, and "we are afraid they will try to eat us all."

The younger braves were in agreement and looking for some excitement. They cried out, "Let's go on the warpath and kill the Indian chief." And so it was decided.

The warriors walked around inside the camp circle of tepees to make medicine, and went out the opening facing east. Then they walked around the outside of the camp facing west, wearing their best war bonnets, clothes, and regalia. They walked all night.

Just before the sun came up, they reached the Indian camp. Then they attacked. The Turtle chief went into the Indian chief's lodge. He took the Indian by surprise, grabbed him by the throat, and choked him until he was dead. Then he bit off his scalp and slipped it under the dead chief's bedding.

Later that morning the Indians found their dead chief. A crier went out through the camp telling the people to watch out for enemies. Later someone moved the chief's bed and saw a strange-looking spot of fresh earth under it. They used a stick and pushed it back and forth and felt something hard. So they pushed some more and discovered the Turtle. They knew then that the Turtle had killed their chief.

The people then had their own council meeting. They wondered what they should do with the Turtle. "Put him in the fire," hollered one man. "No," said another, "he won't burn right because his shell is too hard."

"Then let's hang him," said another. "No, I think we should cut off his head," said a fourth man. "No," said a fifth man, "I have a better idea. Let's drown him." Everyone agreed that this was the best way.

So that day they took the Turtle to the pond to perform a ceremony and drown him. The whole village came out to see, and one of the special warriors was chosen to drown the Turtle. This man was painted with war paint.

He carried the Turtle out into the pond and waded into deeper water. The Turtle acted like he was scared and tried to get loose. Just as the man was starting to put the Turtle in the water, it turned and bit him. The man hollered and fell into the water, whereupon Turtle drowned him and bit off his scalp.

The people waited, and when the man didn't come to the surface of the water, they didn't know what to do. They were afraid to go into the water, so they all just left. The Turtle stayed in the pond until night came; then he went back to the Indian camp and hunted until he found the chief's scalp. He was so quiet and had so much power that he could sneak past anyone unnoticed. He was proud that he had taken two scalps by himself. Then he went home and told his friends, but said: "Maybe one day the Indians will be our friends and we will share some of our secrets about power with them, just as long as they don't eat us anymore."

In the catalog of animal symbols above, I haven't included every sign in Nature, but I do want you to realize that the appearance of something in Nature going out of its way to get our attention is significant. It is not just a coincidence, and it is therefore up to you to figure out its meaning.

Nature communicates to us, and we can learn how to communicate with it and can learn from its symbolic communication. Knowledge of Nature's symbols requires an awareness, open mind, time to study and learn, and a desire to see the meaning and value of this kind of knowledge. According to traditional Native American philosophy, nothing is coincidental, and everything happens for a reason. I wouldn't advise carrying the concept of omens to an extreme and thinking that every movement in Nature means something. On the other hand, I think a broader scope of perception and a deeper understanding of Nature and our relations can help us to gain a better understanding of the world around us. In turn, this kind of unique knowledge can serve to increase our intuitive development and our personal intelligence. In some situations it just might save our lives, as has been the case with me on numerous occasions.

Remember, if an animal, bird, or one of our other relations in Nature goes out of its way to get your attention, you can assume that there is a special message and meaning involved. Wild creatures do not belong in your house, so if one should suddenly appear in the house, act accordingly. It has definitely gone out of its normal path to visit you, and to call something to your attention! On the other hand, if you decide to drive to the state park and look at a herd of Buffalo, the appearance of one or more Buffalo might not mean anything. Or if you go to Florida and visit an Alligator farm, you should expect to see Alligators.

This concept is partly built into the Western tradition, as in the annual ritual that has evolved around Ground Hog Day, or the return of the Swallows to Capistrano. Certain communities and small cities have an annual celebration, as a means of welcoming the coming of spring and the ending of winter.

Recent scientific efforts by geologists to study the behavior of bugs, birds, and animals in an effort to predict earthquakes and other potential natural disasters is an example of how mythic-symbolic knowledge can gain credibility and be of value to Western society.

Here is documented evidence and an example of how I tried to use Nature's language to help the people in my home area. When I was living in California, I wrote a letter to the editor of the *Arcata Union*; it appeared on November 28, 1985:

Editor:

Certain signs in Nature clearly indicate that we are going to have a harsh and long winter. The unusual behavior of fish, birds, animals, bugs, and erratic weather patterns all serve as "omens" forewarning the possibility of a major flood—perhaps even worse than the 1964 floods. For example, Sharks and Porpoises have been seen going up the local rivers, and according to our Native beliefs, this is a very bad sign. Such omens warn of potential floods which could impact the Trinity, Klamath, Smith, Mad, and Eel rivers sometime this late winter or early spring. Consider it fantasy or fact, what if this is true? What is being done locally to prepare for such a potential disaster?

History should teach us lessons and we should learn from our mistakes. Why wait until after the disaster to enact "emergency measures"? Has the Hoopa Tribal Council developed a natural disaster plan and established an emergency fund? Has the Bureau of Indian Affairs considered the possibility of the effect of a natural or national disaster upon the Indian-federal lands, and has this agency established a plan and fund to deal with such a potential problem? What about the County Board of Supervisors—are they going to wait until the last minute and then complain about budget deficits, or wait until "after" the disaster strikes just so they can "qualify" for supplemental funds? And what about the local Native residents along the rivers—are they prepared to handle such a calamity?

What if the Hoopa Medical Clinic and Hospital is wiped out—do we have an emergency medical team or group of Native healers on reserve and ready to handle an emergency? What if the water systems, sewage systems, stores, roads, PG&E [Pacific Gas and Electric] were all devastated—are the people and agencies prepared to move the injured, hurt, sick, and scared to a predesignated safe facility with reserve supplies? Has a volunteer rescue team been established to deal with such a potential disaster? And what about families, neighbors, and friends—are they prepared to deal with a disaster, or committed to help each other, or will they wait until the last minute and then panic?

Consider me a fool or a friend, all I ask is that you all consider the above information and make your own decision about what I have tried to share.

Just weeks after the letter appeared, numerous rain- and snowstorms struck Northern California. There were twenty-four inches of rain and nine feet of snow. Twelve thousand people fled their homes. A bridge collapsed, a huge mud slide closed a major highway, homes were flooded, and people died. The storms caused tens of millions of dollars in damage.

Using Nature's Symbols

Creating a Medicine Shield

▼▼▼▼▼▼▼▼▼▼▼▼▼

I would now like to teach you the symbolic meaning and purpose of the medicine wheel and how it is used in some Native American tribal-cultural practices. Refer to the following examples of the medicine wheel. Study them carefully. Try to close your eyes and absorb the ancient symbol or archetype into your subconscious mind. You might want to make one of your own that you can put in a meditation room to use as a power symbol for self-hypnosis during meditation, or that you can place over the head of your bed for protection against bad dreams or negative forces.

You can also make the medicine wheel into a medicine shield. The intent of the shield is to have a "natural" symbol and power object that reflects your own chosen powers and symbols from Nature. This symbol in turn can be used for protection. A long time ago, the White

people in Europe and other races and cultures in other countries had what they called "family emblems" and "war shields." Remember the Roman soldiers, the Knights of the Round Table, the Crusaders, and even so-called barbarians? They all had shields and emblems with symbols from Nature, such as the Lion, Eagle, or Bear.

Now get some material to make your own medicine wheel. It can be made out of a small tree sapling and leather, or you can decide to draw or paint one on a large piece of cardboard or canvas. If you decide to make one from a tree sapling in the woods near a creek, then get the wood during fall, when the sap has already dried up but is still flexible. Bend it into a circle shape, then tie and glue it. Cut out a large piece of leather and stretch it over the hoop, then punch holes in it and lace it tight. You can buy dry pieces of rawhide from certain arts-and-crafts stores, or use tanned hide if you so desire. The leather can be purchased from taxidermy shops. In either case the intent is to use the material to make a "shield" which reconnects you with the powers in Nature and the ancient, primal, and natural symbols in your own subconscious mind.

After you have completed the structure of the shield, I want you to sit down somewhere in Nature and meditate. Close your eyes and think of four specific powers/symbols/archetypes from Nature that appeal to you the most, or four specific powers you have seen the most, physically or in dreams. These can be birds, animals, snakes, bugs, reptiles, whatever. Be creative in your symbolic work here. Your medicine shield should be divided into four sections, to represent the four elements, the four colors, and the four powers of Creation. Place a different natural power for each separate direction, either on the inside circle of your shield or at a precise point on the outside. You can even hang feathers or other special power objects and symbols from it if you want. This is now your personal medicine wheel and medicine shield. It has a dual purpose and a multifaceted meaning. Remember, the circle is holy and has power in it, so this shield reflects your personal power or your personal desire for certain spirit guides and protectors.

Hang the shield up in your front room, bedroom, or meditation room. Use it as a symbol for developing creative-symbolic thinking and protection. Ask the new symbol to protect you from all evil, bad dreams, bad luck, bad people, and sickness. Find a few moments regularly to sit down and stare at it, meditate with a cedar or sage smudging, and visualize this symbol in you and all around you. In time and with practice, you will sense empowerment because this experiment serves to awaken the creative intelligence you have kept dormant. It reactivates the latent archetypal images of the Earth that are in the unconscious part of your mind, and it becomes another connecting agent between Nature and you.

I have used the same concept and practice here as a form of

therapy in helping both Native American and non-Indian people deal with their mental, physical, emotional, and spiritual problems. Some of these people were trying to find ways to get rid of the past hurts, pain, abuses, habits, violations, and subconscious negative symbols and forces that had put them out of balance in life. The philosophy, construction, and symbolic-spiritual use of the medicine shield served to replace their negative thoughts and symbols with positive, creative, and spiritual symbols and forces. It empowered and offered protection to those who were searching for a way to counteract fear, shame, insecurity, and low self-esteem. This knowledge can also have a therapeutic and healing effect on you if used properly and with respect.

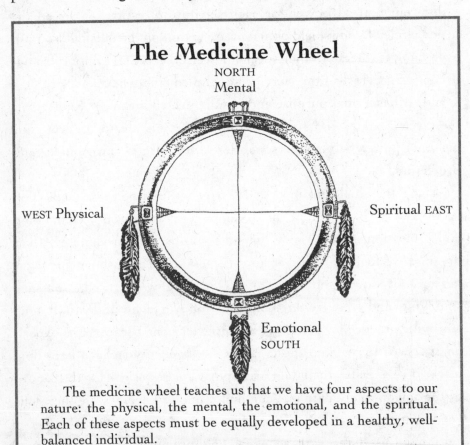

The Medicine Wheel

NORTH
Mental

WEST Physical

Spiritual EAST

Emotional
SOUTH

The medicine wheel teaches us that we have four aspects to our nature: the physical, the mental, the emotional, and the spiritual. Each of these aspects must be equally developed in a healthy, well-balanced individual.

An Exercise to Develop Creative and Symbolic Dreaming

▼▼▼▼▼▼▼▼▼▼▼▼▼▼▼▼▼▼▼▼▼▼▼▼▼▼▼▼▼

Native American people in many different tribes have historically and traditionally assigned special importance to dreams. In addition, a considerable number of psychologists, including Freud, Fromm, and Jung, have studied the phenomenon extensively, each putting forward his own concept of how to interpret dreams, how to use dreams for psychoanalysis, and how dreams affect mental balance in a positive or negative way.

Dr. Patricia Garfield, a leading authority on dreams and dreaming, made these comments about the benefits of creative dreaming:

> As you succeed in establishing creative dreaming, you will be achieving a lifetime victory. You will increase your capacity for concentration and recall. You will build a capacity for coping with fear-producing dream situations that carries over into the waking state. You will experience pleasurable adventures in your dreams. You will understand yourself better. You will help define and unify the unique personality that is you. You will find support and help for waking problems. You will be able to produce things of usefulness and beauty that both express yourself and enrich the world. And all this may be just the beginning.

As an example, let us for a moment remember the famous scientist Friedrich Kekulé, who tried for many years to determine the molecular structure of benzene. He reported dreaming as he dozed in front of a fireplace and from his unconscious mind emerged the vision of a Snake eating its own tail, thus forming a circle. Kekulé realized that the structure of benzene was a closed carbon ring. This was a significant discovery that revolutionized modern chemistry. While presenting his theory before a large convention of scientists and scholars, he concluded: "Let us dream, gentlemen, and then we may perhaps find the truth."

In earlier times, prior to the European invasion, indigenous people used creative dreaming as a regular part of their life. Medicine men/women, or what Western people call shamans, were the leaders in this knowledge; and they are still keepers of that knowledge today.

Chief Luther Standing Bear remarked decades ago: "The man who sat on the ground in his tepee meditating on life, intuition, and its meaning, accepting the kinship of all creatures and acknowledging unity with the Universe of things, was infusing into his being the true essence of civilization." And a significant number of American Indian people on and off the reservation still consult "medicine people" about their dreams. So there evidently appears to be some common unconscious symbols relating to dream belief, practice, and utilization, although they may vary somewhat from one Native American tribe or community to another.

The objective of this dream information and these exercises are to provide you with basic knowledge concerning the value of creative dreaming as a means of helping you to become more aware of the "natural" symbols in your subconscious mind; to figure out what certain natural symbols mean when they appear in your dreams and how to use this creative dreaming and thinking activity as a way of developing your innate intuitive spiritual powers. By learning how to work with the right hemisphere of your mind-brain complex, you will be developing a more holistic perspective and understanding of life, which in turn should create more balance in your life. The information presented here is not intended to provide you with an in-depth account of dreaming, which would require a book in itself and many years of study, guidance, and practice. What I intend to share here is more of a basic introduction to the concept of dreaming in hopes of helping you to become more aware of the natural symbols as they appear in your dreams, and enabling you to interpret the dreams by using the guide on natural symbols provided in the chapter called "Nature's Symbols."

A number of years ago, when my daughter was only about eight months old, she was sleeping with my wife and me instead of in her crib. At the time my wife Tela had very long hair which extended down past her waistline. On this particular night she had a very disturbing dream. She dreamed she saw a baby Hawk trying to fly with its mother. In the dream it appeared to be weak, not capable of keeping up, and was about to start falling toward the ground. Then my wife heard the mother Hawk tell her, in the dream, "Wake up, sister, wake up. Your baby is in trouble." She could hear the Hawk screaming.

Tela woke up immediately from the dream, scared and bewildered. Then she started hollering at me and made me wake up. Tela's long hair had somehow gotten wrapped around our infant daughter's throat. I calmed my wife and began to pray while I reached over for a pocket knife on the end table and proceeded to cut and unravel the hair. Luckily, our baby was not injured and weathered the accident with no side effects, but we were very shaken. As we sat on the side of the bed praying and smudging up the infant, we heard the scream of a Hawk, who was sitting out on the apartment balcony and remained there until our infant calmed down and appeared to be safe and secure. In our Native way we thanked that Red-tailed Hawk, and we have continually made prayers and food offerings to the Hawk people as our daughter and our other children have grown up. Obviously, if we did not know what the symbol meant, if my wife had ignored the dream, then in all probability our daughter would have died. So to us, this kind of ancient knowledge is invaluable, and it still works in modern life, even in an urban setting.

By learning how to become a creative dreamer, you will develop specific skills to achieve a level of attention and ability to concentrate. The creative dreaming method can help you sustain dream images for long periods of time until you begin to understand the symbols and what they mean to you personally, culturally, and spiritually. As you develop the skill, you will find that your memory in the conscious state will improve and become more vivid. Ultimately, and with a dedication to practice, you will be able to focus your attention on those aspects of your dreams that interest you and retain clear visual images of them. But you should understand that you might not be able to "see" and remember your dreams every night, although most people do actually dream every night. Therefore, the skills of attention, focused concentration, memory, and intuitive management will carry over into your daily life, conscious thinking, and work activity and can lead to a lifetime of study.

There are a number of concepts we can learn from Native American cultural systems about dreams:

1. Dreams and dreaming are a significant part of our Native American heritage and culture. We should be proud of them, and we should learn how to use them as a tool for self-discovery, self-esteem building, and for creative-critical thinking and spiritual development.

2. We should regard dreams as important in our lives and learn how to use ancient forms of cultural knowledge as a means of cultivating and developing dream skills and competency, which in turn will help develop our human intelligence.

3. You can create a positive image of yourself in dreams, and this will promote self-esteem, self-confidence, good health, and balance. Take time out in your life to read and study ancient myths and Indian stories before going to bed at night. This will help you set the stage in your unconscious mind for dreaming.

4. A person can learn how to reward themselves in dreaming, as our Native American medicine men/women have done for centuries.

For example, in many tribal societies "dreamers" were given honoring ceremonies and special recognition for a dream that was shared and benefited the community.

5. You can find dream "friends," spirits, and "Nature" symbols in your dreams who can act as messengers, advisers, and guardians to help you during times of fear, frustration, conflict, confusion, or sickness. Our ancient Native American myths, legends, and Nature stories provide the symbols and friends, or what Jung called archetypes, to help us. The more we study, learn, and remember about these stories, the more natural symbols we will strengthen, develop, and use in our mind. Sometimes our relations in Nature try to communicate to us during our waking hours but we don't understand. Oftentimes they will try to follow up this communication by visiting us in our dreams; or we can use creative dreaming techniques as a means of trying to interpret the daytime encounter we had with a creature from Nature.

6. You can create a ritual and an environment for dreaming by finding a quiet place in your own home or out in Nature, or by using the sweat lodge and Moontime ceremonies. Certain tribes even use special places in Nature, including caves, waterfalls, mountains, alpine lakes, and meadows, known as sacred sites and power centers for this purpose. There you smudge yourself for purification, rid your mind and the personal space of all negative energies and potential influences, and calm your mind and soul so as to become receptive to dreaming. Sage and cedar ward off bad spirits and negative energies; sweet grass attracts the good forces and spirits. Learn how to use the ancient and sacred herbs while practicing dreaming.

7. Certain power objects help us in dreaming, such as the sacred Eagle or Hawk feather, a quartz crystal, a rock, or different herbs such as sage or mugwort, a personal medicine bundle, or a talisman. These "tangible" objects help us to believe in and connect with the "intangible." Some tribes also use music to help them get into the

mental mood for dreaming; they sing songs and play drums, rattles, and flutes. Chamomile and hops herbal tea taken before sleep also helps relax the mind and put one in the mental mood for creative dreaming; coffee, alcohol, and drugs deter it.

According to spiritual custom and law, the power objects must be treated with respect and taken care of properly. Otherwise a person could have a negative reaction. For example, you might find a Deer antler in Nature, a snake skin, certain bird feathers, a Turtle shell, or an animal claw, tooth, or hide. Our Native American people consider the objects sacred and treat them with respect. The items are kept in a cedarwood box or trunk and only brought out for meditation and ritual. Some people put the power objects on an altar. We never keep our power objects in the bedroom, hung up on the front-room walls for museum-type display, or lying around anyplace. We are taught to periodically clean the objects by smudging them with cedar, sage, or sweet grass. We sprinkle water upon them to purify them and sometimes we leave a bowl of food such as cornmeal, acorn meal, or oatmeal to feed the spirit and strengthen the power of the object. In some tribes such as the Blackfeet, Cheyenne, and Crow, these items are considered medicine bundles. In other tribes the power objects are considered ceremonial and dance ritual regalia, or shamanistic regalia; hence the objects have historically been hidden from public view and only brought out and used on special occasions for doctoring, ritual, or ceremony. Pregnant women, women during their menses, sick and injured people, and little children were not allowed to be near or touch these objects because it could cause them spiritual, emotional, and physical illness, bad luck, or injury. Power operates on an ancient natural law of cause and effect: for every action there is a reaction. Thus, we are taught to handle our power objects with respect and cleanliness; otherwise the positive could turn into a negative reaction.

(For more information about this in relation to sickness, health, and healing, refer to my book *Native Healer*.)

8. Try to develop a habit and skill of remembering songs you might receive from a dream because one could become your "dream song." Such a song in turn can become the key to your unconscious; it can be used to put you mentally in the mood for dreaming, as in a hypnotic state. It can be used as your secret passport into the reality of dreaming, and your way back into the world of consciousness if you happen to get lost in a dream. A dream song can even be used as a protection song when you feel threatened, scared, sick, or insecure.

9. Also try to remember any gifts you receive from a dream, such as a power object or a talking animal or bird, a rock or a plant. Such a gift from the dream world we Native people call "personal medicine." In the dream it is a symbol, and as we have seen in the earlier chapters of this book, symbols have meaning and power. Sometimes what we see in a dream can manifest itself in physical reality. For example, lots of times I have had dreams about Ravens, Eagles, Hawks, Bears, and Turtles. Shortly afterward I found feathers from these dream allies while walking around in Nature, or friends and relatives gave me feathers, claws, teeth, and shells without my asking. I knew then that the dream objects had found a way to come to me in the physical reality, which in turn encouraged me to have more faith in the purpose and power of dreams.

10. Use the list of signs and omens I have provided (in the earlier chapters of this book) as a guide to help you in dreaming. Learn to use dream friends and allies as supernatural aids to protect you from bad dreams and nightmares, or negative things that challenge you in dreams; learn to use the smudging ritual described below and prayer to develop confidence in protecting yourself from bad dreams, or as a means of keeping bad dreams from coming true. In other words, if you have a bad dream that you, a family member, or a friend is going to get

hurt, say, in a car accident, then perform the smudge ceremony and pray against it; pray to the Great Creator, the good spirits, and your dream friends to change the negative situation into a positive one. Ask the Great Spirit and the good dream allies to prevent the bad dream from coming true. In this way you will be learning how to develop the more positive aspects of the mind in using premonitions.

11. Here is a guide you can use to create an actual ritual designed to develop your dreaming. Just before you get ready to go to bed, bring out your smudge bowl to burn cedar or use a sage smudge stick. (Some of these items can be acquired in New Age–type bookstores and health stores.) Make the room and your house as quiet as possible. Now light the cedar or sage, offer it to the Great Creator, the four directions of the Universe, and to the Mother Earth and our relations in Nature. Take four or five deep breaths, inhale slowly, and then, with eyes closed, slowly count backwards from seven to one while exhaling. Try to re-create a special place you have visited in Nature, reliving or remaking it in your mind while the cedar or sage incense is burning, and use the powers of your mind to visualize an animal, bird, snake, fish, or whatever from Nature. Smell the environment, try to feel the environment around you, and wait for your spirit ally or dream ally to come and visit you. Now, when you see it coming, don't be afraid. Talk to it, ask it to sit down with you and be your teacher. This might take several nights of practice before you can get the visualization right. Now, while you are in a semihypnotized state, ask your spirit ally from Nature to come and visit you in a dream, to show you an answer to a particular problem or to tell you what the sign/omen meant that you saw that day or from a former dream. After 15 to 20 minutes of the ritual, go to bed and dream. The dream guide you create could include certain animals and birds that you have placed on your medicine wheel/shield and to which you feel a special connection.

The more you work with this ritual, the more vivid it will become.

It takes practice. Upon waking up first thing in the morning, get in the habit of writing down or tape-recording the new information and experience you have gained from your dreams. Eventually you will develop your skill.

An Earth-Healing Ceremony

The Earth-Healing Ceremony is an ancient ceremony that can be done individually or in a group as a means of communicating with Nature and bonding with the Earth, and as a way to make restitution to all our relations in Nature. It can be done on a weekly basis, or on a more ritualistic basis on the spring equinox, summer solstice, fall equinox, and winter solstice. I have been performing this ancient ceremony for years, all across the nation, when I give lectures and training workshops. People of all races, cultures, and religions seem to really like it and appreciate it. But before I detail the ceremony, let me tell you a short story illustrating how and why it is done.

This past year I went to the Theosophical Society in Wheaton to conduct a workshop on Nature's symbolic language, a discussion similar to what I have been trying to share in this book. A couple of friends of mine, John and Carole, let me stay in their apartment in

Chicago. John's friend Carole offered her bedroom to me (instead of putting me in a motel), which I thought was very kind and respectful, but I would have been just as grateful to have slept on the couch. Anyway, I didn't get much sleep that night. I was in torment all night long. I kept having dreams about a Monkey running around with no head, a Rattlesnake trying to crawl into the bed and bite me on the foot, and an Owl trying to attack me. The next morning I got up tired, irritable, groggy, and with aches and pains in my head, feet, and body. When John and Carole asked me how I'd slept, I felt a little embarrassed to tell the truth. But knowing that the dreams and torment happened for a reason, I told them. There was an important symbolic message in this dream which in turn could lead to healing.

Carole became quite disturbed and embarrassed but openly admitted that she had these items in her bedroom. She had the skull of a Monkey, a Rattlesnake skin and tail, and the Snake was carefully laid under an Owl's wing, all of which were at the foot of her bed, out of sight. She had found these different items over the years or people had given them to her, and in her own way she had considered the items as power objects, and as part of her connection to Nature. Upon further discussion I discovered that she had been experiencing arthritis, headaches, and sleeplessness—the same symptoms I'd picked up that night while sleeping in her bedroom.

So I told her that the power objects were causing her torment since she had not acquired the items in a proper and spiritual way. The symbols were having a negative effect upon her because they had not "chosen" to work with her as spirit allies or powers, and she had these things near her while menstruating. (Refer to my book *Native Healer* for more information on this concept and the relationship of menses to power and healing.) To make matters worse, the Rattlesnake and Owl, in spirit symbol and power form, were at battle with each other. Thus, I suggested (as a prescription provided in *Native Healer*) that she

make restitution by giving the objects back to Nature and by partici-
pating in an Earth-Healing Ceremony to confess her violations against
Nature so as to eliminate the causes of her illness and in a natural way
get back into balance with Nature and her life. She agreed, performed
the ceremony, and has not had any further problems. Some of you
who have a similar problem might learn from the above example and
wish to perform the following exercise:

According to ancient custom and law, it is against the natural law
of the Creator and the Universe to kill, torment, and mishandle our
relations in Nature without just cause. If handled in a bad way, the
power and symbols can have a negative effect upon our lives. In the
Indian way, we usually perform a ritual, and ask the spirits for permission to use their body and powers. For example, we ask the animals
and birds, whom we also consider to be spirits, if we can use their
hides, heads, claws, bones, feathers, and so forth, for rituals and ceremonies. We do not use such items as trophies or simply for display,
because we believe everything on the Earth is sacred. Therefore, each
item should be treated with respect, in recognition of the fact that it
has purpose and function.

Thus, if one has violated the natural laws, and the powers show up
in our dreams, we have an opportunity to redeem ourselves, make
restitution, and balance our "karmic" debt, so to speak, by giving the
objects back to Nature in a ceremonial way, and by confessing our vio-
lation and making restitution by offering tobacco or cornmeal in an
Earth-Healing Ceremony. This serves to cleanse not only the conscious mind but also the spirit. And it helps us develop a closer kinship
with, and consideration for, our relations in Nature, who in turn often
come to listen to what we are saying and doing. So don't be surprised
if Crows or some other birds or animals show up while you are performing the ceremony, or if more creatures start coming closer to you
in your daily life thereafter. They need our prayers in order to survive,

and they also need our protection if their species, and our species, are to survive together on the Earth.

Earth-Healing Ceremony

1. Find a private and quiet place in Nature and build a small sacred fire. First, put rocks in a circle to represent all of Creation and the holiness of life and the Universe, because the symbol of the circle serves to help bond us with Nature.

2. Next, take small pieces of wood and shape them into an altar or a tepee, then light your fire on the eastern-door side, as is done in all our Native rituals and ceremonies.

3. Stand and offer tobacco to the Great Spirit, the four powers/directions of the Universe, and the Mother Earth, then place it in the fire and pray.

4. Say something like this: "Great Spirit, Mother Earth, and all my relations in nature, we come before you in a humble manner, and according to the ancient custom and law, we offer this tobacco to you. We ask that you forgive us for mishandling the [name whatever power object or natural item it was], and we are sorry we did that out of ignorance. We have returned those items [name whatever they are] back to the woods and in a private part of Nature.*

"We pray for a healing of this Earth, we pray for all our relations in Nature, and we give thanks for this beautiful world. We ask that our relations in Nature, all those that walk, crawl, fly, and swim, accept us into the Great Circle of Creation, and that they communicate to us in our daily lives and in our dreams. Thank you."

*Do not burn power objects in the sacred fire. Either bury them in Nature or just lay them in a private place out of view of other people and say: "You come from the Earth and I return you to the Earth to be recycled. Please do not torment me anymore."

Power Centers and
Sacred Places

From the very Beginning of Creation there have been "power centers." Our elders teach us that the Great Creator made such places for a reason and a purpose. Ancient myths and stories teach us that power centers are sacred places where the spirits and alleged "gods" reside, while some religious doctrines reveal that specific, newer centers are where one goes to make direct contact with the Great Spirit that flows through all life, seen and unseen. Such places are sacred and holy; hence they should be respected, protected, preserved, and used properly.

The best-known power centers in a global sense are Mount Sinai, the Great Pyramids of Egypt, Stonehenge, Machu Picchu, the Mayan Temples, Mount Fuji, the Black Hills, and the Himalayan Mountains, just to name a few popular sites. On the North American continent, the more notable sites include, but are not limited to, Bear Butte and Devil's Tower, Mount Shasta, Dawn Blue Lake, the Four Corners area, the

San Francisco Peaks, the Black Hills, Chief Mountain, the Allegheny Mountains, Niagara Falls, the Cascades, Grandfather Mountain/Great Smoky Mountains, Chimney Rock, Lake Tahoe, Crater Lake, Upper Priest Lake, Flathead Lake, Mount Rainier, Doctor Rock, Chimney Rock in northwestern California, the Marble Mountains, the Trinity Alps, the ancient Redwood Forests, and Mount Chuchama/Tecate near San Diego. (Refer to W. Y. Evans-Wentz, *Cuchama and the Sacred Mountains*, for a better understanding and a more comprehensive list of power centers worldwide.)

What I would like to share with you here is my own spiritual view and explanation of the power centers as I have come to understand them over thirty-plus years of shamanistic training in such places by over sixteen different medicine elders from different tribes.

I have previously shared in detail one of my own spiritual experiences concerning a very sacred and powerful mountain used by the Native American people in northwestern California. This site has been controversial for over two decades due to the conflict over its ownership and legal use between the U.S. Forest Service and the Native tribes. The Sierra Club and the Audubon Society have sided with the Native people in this dispute. But there are other power centers on our Turtle Island both small and large, low and high, dry and wet, whose power is either positive or negative, neutral, or both.

Willard Park's *Shamanism in Western North America* and Joan Halifax's *Shamanic Voices* offer a variety of examples illustrating how the different kinds of power centers are used by different kinds of shamans from different geographical regions. The more classic and detailed examples, however, can be found in the works of Alfred L. Kroeber, Cora DuBois, Mircea Eliade, Lowell Bean, and Thomas Buckley. This literature can provide a serious base of study for those who are searching for ways in which Native American people have actually pursued, acquired, and applied varying degrees of power

179

from specific kinds of power centers, which include mountains, alpine lakes, caves, waterfalls, forests, prairie mounds, plateaus, rivers, and ocean sites.

It is important to study these works because one can learn not only the significance and meaning of the power center but also how to approach and utilize the power center in a spiritual and proper manner, instead of trespassing on it, as many people are doing today. For example, some of the larger mountains, such as Mount Shasta and Mount Saint Helens, were not used for vision quests and power training by the indigenous people not because the Indians lacked sophisticated mountain climbing skills, but because they "knew" exactly what kind of power was there and the reason it was there. Ella Clark explains that Native people recognized certain mountains not as the home of spirits and gods but as a giant spirit in the hierarchy of Earth spirits. My elders have taught me that such places are where the Great Creator resides from time to time. Thus, the people are not supposed to trespass on this kind of power center because it is too powerful. It is too holy. Most humans are not pure enough to qualify to go there and meet the Great Creator directly, in His abode.

A power center is the residence of a special spirit being who is high in status in the hierarchy. Other power centers are the home of a particular family of spirits. Such entities have been placed on this Earth from the very Beginning of Creation for a purpose and a reason. They have a specific job to perform for the Great Creator. As a result, these spirits either serve to create that source of power and energy or guard, maintain, perpetuate, and use that power center as the basis for their purpose and function. The spirits who reside within or comprise that power center adhere to and are governed by a system of natural laws. The laws are both spiritual and physical. These spirits or entities are both physical and spiritual. Their existence, the Earth's existence, and our existence are dependent upon maintaining the natural laws in a harmonious state of balance. The law of physics, for example, states that for every action there is a reaction. This same concept applies to both the physical and spiritual dimensions (or if you cannot relate to this analogy, think of it in terms of matter and energy). Traditional Native ideology provides us with a warning: Anytime human beings interfere with, violate, or alter the power center, they are causing a serious imbalance; hence a negative and detrimental reaction can occur.

Native people or shamans from other parts of the world who intend to approach and utilize a specific power center therefore prepare themselves properly. They demonstrate respect and protocol by purifying their body, mind, and soul of all negative influences and/or energies by use of ritual cleansing, fasting, and prayer. For example, the practitioner might bathe in herbs such as sage or angelica root, steam him/herself with Douglas fir boughs in an open pit, or use the sacred sweat lodge, a hot spring, a waterfall, or some kind of ceremonial lodge, depending upon the individual's cultural background and belief. In traditional Native cultures, the practitioner normally uses the sweat lodge as a means of preparing. While in the lodge, he/she makes an invocation to the Great Creator and the spirit of the power center to be visited, and asks for permission to go on a quest to the power center. He/she abstains from sex, drugs, alcohol, and any possible blood contamination via women's menses, meat, physical wounds, or deceased people. He/she waits for a sign or omen. If none is received, then he/she will not visit the power center or will postpone it until a later date. The preparation ritual normally lasts four days prior to the visit, and another three to four days after leaving the power center. Why?

The period of abstinence afterward is for protection. The practitioner believes that the spirit from the mountain will follow him/her home and answer prayers, and so does not want to break the connection. In other situations the practitioner might be infused with power and energy. It takes time for the human body to mentally, emotionally, physically, and spiritually adjust to the new power, to study a dream, or to interpret a vision. The practitioner believes that power flows both ways, and does not want to break this connection. There is another variable worth noting here and it has to do with "energy vibrations." When a person receives power from a power center, it raises their vibratory level, and it takes time for the human mind/body/soul complex to adjust to this new vibratory level. If this vibratory process is interfered with or contaminated, the practitioner could become seriously injured or ill. I have personally doctored some people who became crippled from the experience because they did not follow the natural laws while "spiritually training" during a power quest.

Another matter I would like to share with you here is the role power centers play in relation to the Mother Earth. This Earth is a living organism (someday Western scientists will discover that reality). Hence the power centers are vital to the life force of the earth, and as such, some power centers might be compared to "psychic centers" or the endocrine glands found in the human body. They therefore serve as "chakras" or vital organs, comparable in purpose and function to the major organs found in the human body, in both their physiological and spiritual aspects.

The smaller power centers might be compared to other parts of the body, such as organs, nerve centers, muscles, joints, arteries, and even cells for that matter. So I ask: What happens to your power, your health, your function, and balance of the mind/body/soul complex when any part becomes disturbed, polluted, violated, or exploited without proper permission, preparation, or application? What if your pineal gland was suddenly removed, or your thyroid gland poisoned? Can you imagine the effect this would have upon your entire endocrine system? Obviously there would be some kind of physical and spiritual, mental and emotional reaction.

By the same token, certain parts of your body also have power centers, which are highly protected by physical and spiritual forces, for example, cells and cellular energies. The purpose and function of the human power centers are to keep the human organism alive and functioning well, to keep it in balance. What would happen to your well-being if one of the body's power centers were interfered with, altered, damaged, or destroyed? And how many of your power centers are irreplaceable? How important are natural minerals, water, air, and energy to the proper functioning of your body's organism and life force? And what effect do positive and negative energy have upon various parts of your own psychic centers?

I am simply trying to find a more humanistic way to help you understand just how vital "power centers" are to this Earth, to all species that are a part of this Earth, and to all living things, both seen and unseen, that are dependent upon this Earth for survival. This Mother Earth is also dependent upon us for her survival.

Thus, there are power centers upon the Earth to which one makes a pilgrimage in order to give, not just to take. Certain holy places are used as specific places allowing us, as humans, to return the power. It is a reciprocal relationship and responsibility. One makes a pilgrimage to pray for the Earth, to give it positive, loving, creative, and nourishing energy. This kind of energy is needed in order to replenish its psychic centers. As a living organism, the Earth needs recharging because it can occasionally become drained. You are part of this Earth, and you draw energies from the Earth. This energy now must be recycled to keep up the life force, to keep it flowing harmoniously. Energy going one way causes a drain, and then eventually a serious depletion.

The ancient, primordial, and contemporary sacred ceremonies and pilgrimages also provide a positive and natural return of power and energy. That is why we, as medicine people, go to certain power centers to pray and give thanks. Our songs, prayers, tobacco, herbs, offerings, cleanliness, fasting, and sacrificing all help to keep Creation alive. Ritualistic pilgrimages to the power centers are a spiritual form of recharging and recycling energy back to its original source. And that is why we stay "clean" when we go to a power center.

A contaminated or negative transmission can harm the power center. It can also cause a harmful backlash. For example, I was taught by the elders to abstain from food, water, alcohol, drugs, and sex and to fast before, during, and after the visit for at least four days. In the traditional Indian way, we also purify ourselves in a sacred sweat lodge or bathe in a hot spring, a waterfall, or a stream.

There are other power centers, such as caves and rock outcroppings, or designated mounds, that are used for seeking a vision, to acquire power or to channel and redirect the power into a person, ceremony, ritual or sacred dance. Charlie Thom, a Karuk medicine man, explains it this way:

> A medicine man must go to the mountain or some other power center to pray for his people. That is his job. I connect with the power and shoot it straight down from the mountaintop into the sacred dance. It is like a beam of light, or electricity. It will make the healing more powerful. It strengthens the dancers. And I ask the spirits from the mountain to come down and dance with us in the ceremony, as our ancestors originally did in the Beginning.

In Matthew 17 in the New Testament of the Bible, we learn that Jesus did the same thing for his people as a means of strengthening his healing power. The original teachings of Jesus as found in the Essenes provides an interesting view on this subject which is similar to the Native belief about the Earth, the powers, and power centers.

There have been many times during my own healing sessions when I felt the power weakening. I was being drained, or the case required stronger power and medicine. In such situations I had to go up a mountain, into a cave, or inside an ancient redwood tree, or visit a sacred waterfall, or use the sweat lodge in order to receive support from the spirits, the Mother Earth, and the Great Creator. In other situations I have gone to a power center to pray and ask for guidance concerning a patient I was doctoring at the time. I pleaded for the spirits and the Great Creator to let the healing power/energy flow stronger through me so I could channel it into the patient. Over the years I have learned that different sicknesses, injuries, and people require different sources of power, energy, and medicine in order to be cured. During the quest, I could feel the power surge through my entire body, the vibration sometimes knocking me unconscious. I could feel the connection in the same way current flows from an electrical outlet. Fasting and abstaining from sex and water, drugs, alcohol, and even certain foods at that time made the current stronger, and the connection lasted longer. In addition to places that provide a religious experience, there are indeed specific places upon this Earth which definitely provide a natural source of healing energy that can be tapped into and transmitted to the self and/or patient.

Certain power centers have different purposes and sources of power, and different degrees of power. There are power centers that Native people have traditionally used to bring rain, such as Rain Rock, or Thunder. There are power centers where Native people have quested in order to become warriors, athletes, fortune-tellers, seers, basket makers, canoe makers, hunters, or doctors. There are "Good-Luck Rocks" to which our Native American people go to pray for good luck in gambling. The power manifests itself in a dream to the quester, or by finding a power object, or by making contact with a ghost that becomes one's spirit ally. Sometimes the power is manifested through an animal, bird, fish, snake, or herb. There are also power centers that are used only by women for visions and spiritual knowledge.

Such places are used as a source of power to cope with life crises during puberty, menses, childbirth, menopause, or loss of a spouse. In all of the above-mentioned examples one can use the power center as a holy place, meaning a quiet and spiritual site where one can pray in privacy to the Great Creator, the Mother Earth, the spirits, and Nature.

Our elders also teach that when such places are violated, the power reacts, first as a warning, then as a penalty. One contemporary example is the case of Mount Saint Helens, although Westerners might disagree with this contention. I suspect that the Western scientist would attempt to explain the power center in terms of thermodynamics, energy magnitude, mineral composition, and geological laws of cause and effect. But this does not explain *why* the power center is powerful per se, physically or psychically, or how the physical and spiritual laws are any different. Perhaps it is just a problem of semantics, and for this reason should be explained more in terms of the traditional Native understanding.

Medicine men/women, shamans from other countries, and spiritual/psychic leaders such as lamas and gurus can make the right connection on a power center and cause lightning, thunder, rain, and even snow on a clear day or night. This has been documented in a number of works, ranging from those of Willard Park to Mircea Eliade and John Niehardt; more recent examples are provided in Doug Boyd on Rolling Thunder, and Wabun Wind on Sun Bear. Jeffrey Goodman defines this phenomenon as a form of "biorelativity." He attempts to explain the power center's electrical potential in relation to mineral alloys and composition, plus atmospheric conditions. Contemporary medicine men such as Wallace Black (Sioux), Charles Thom (Karuk), Archie Fire Lame Deer (Lakota), or Thomas Banayca (Hopi) explain the process and connection in spiritual knowledge, while medicine women such as Flora Jones (Wintun), and Tela Starhawk Lake (Yurok-Karuk-Hupa), speaking from a female perspective, concur. In either case, it would behoove us to realize that there is indeed something very special about the power centers, and something incredible about the shamans who know how to connect with the power and apply it in weather control, healing, ceremony, ritual, agriculture, survival, or protection. No matter how many people in Western society scoff at the idea, such shamans have been using power centers to invoke rain, wind, and snow and to ward off droughts for thousands of years. And some still do. This "something special" I am talking about is the knowledge and experience that the medicine man/woman/shaman has of the power center and his/her innate ability to connect with and utilize this power while other humans cannot.

I hope we may come to have greater respect for those power centers as the environment continues to degrade with each passing year. But I hope it won't require physical evidence of natural disasters before Western society begins to realize the significance of these power centers, because by then it might be too late to preserve and protect the sites or appreciate the people who still know how to use the power centers for the sake of humanity.

Most people in Western society recognize the worth of a power center in monetary terms, meaning the value of minerals such as gold, or the natural resources it can provide, such as timber, gas, water, and wind. There are exceptions to this view, however, among those who seem to appreciate the aesthetic and natural beauty of power centers. Such a minority from Western society should be commended for their efforts to preserve the power centers as natural and historic resources, either tribal or national. But I would like to carry such people a step further and help them to realize the true spiritual value of the power centers for what they really are: a source of power—essentially, a natural place that has physical, mental, emotional, and spiritual power (energy) beyond economic value.

Power centers have been established upon this Earth from the Beginning of Creation. Many of the sites are still active and are being used today by Native American people in various parts of the country, and by esoteric practitioners in other countries around the world. The power centers have a specific purpose and function. They are located in specific geographical places for a specific reason and purpose. While this may seem like a far-fetched metaphysical statement, some of our traditional Native people believe that certain power centers are actually doorways to other dimensions. And some of the power centers are negative sources of power, being the residences of bad spirits, forces, and energies.

All of the power centers, regardless of their purpose and function, should be respected. Power centers used by Native tribal groups and individuals should not be interfered with, violated, damaged, destroyed, or confiscated by those in Western society who see only the economic value of the land. The continued economic exploitation of the Earth's vital power centers is causing a very serious imbalance worldwide which can no longer be ignored. Weird weather patterns, volcanic eruptions, increased earthquake activity, record-breaking snowstorms, floods, droughts, pestilence, and new diseases are all possible negative outcomes. Such phenomena are evidence that the power centers are being violated. The Mother Earth is not only becoming polluted but she is also becoming weak and very sick. Her "psychic" centers are seriously damaged and need healing. In order to be healed, the sites must be protected and preserved. If she dies, we all die; it is as simple as that. Thus, what I have tried to present here is not a metaphysical and romantic notion but a different form of truth and reality.

Relearning Nature's
Language

Native American and indigenous peoples have historically demonstrated a tremendous amount of reverence for Nature and all of Creation. The "traditional" Native Americans, ceremonial leaders, and medicine people still relate to the world in a spiritual way, despite the effects of genocide, acculturation, and assimilation on their heritage and culture. They see the world as a great mystery, full of magic, mysticism, challenge, and liveliness. And because it is alive, it communicates to us. The ancient philosophy and ideology of Native American people provide us with a perspective that is critically lacking in Western society, a worldview that reminds us that mankind is not separate from Nature, and that everything in Nature is our relation. Within this universal kinship exists an ancient language, a language that is symbolic, natural, spiritual, and still relevant. The ancient symbols and meanings are recorded in myth, litera-

ture, ritual, ceremony, and Nature stories, and they can be found in the deeper levels of our unconscious mind.

For many people, the language will need to be relearned, and they will, no doubt, have difficulty trying to relearn it. The key to understanding the language depends upon one's relationship to the Earth, Nature, and life itself. The kind of relationship a person has with the Earth also shapes his or her perspective and value system with respect to the Earth and Nature. That is why I believe Native American myths and Nature stories are so important. They serve to link us with the environment in which we live; they provide us with a natural description of the Earth; and they teach us Nature's symbolic language. This is turn provides us with a better understanding of Nature in general.

This kind of knowledge may be ancient but it is not archaic. It still has value and meaning today. How can we tell? Because the Falcon can be seen flying around skyscrapers in New York City; the Coyote has been known to come down to visit people in their backyard in Phoenix and Los Angeles; the Eagle still flies over Seattle; and not too long ago a Moose and a Bear had to be relocated from a shopping mall in Spokane, Washington. A Whale was seen for weeks in the river in downtown Sacramento; a Cougar was found in the suburbs of San Francisco. Snakes, Lizards, Frogs, and birds mysteriously appear in college administration buildings, while Ravens and Seagulls, Hawks and Owls can even be seen within the isolated walls of a prison.

Are such sightings simply a coincidence, or is there actually a synchronistic message and meaning involved? Does Nature really have a complex and multifaceted intelligence of its own, or is it a question of our imagination running wild? Do Native Americans project animism upon inanimate objects, or are they actually perceiving the innate reality of things in Nature? And what if the world is really full of spirits, as the traditional Native American people claim—how does that reality affect our own perceptions, values, and behavior in relation to the Earth and Nature?

A well-known Stoney Indian leader, Tatanga Mani (Walking Buffalo), stated at the age of eighty-seven during the late 1960s:

> We may have been considered lawless people, but we were on pretty good terms with the Great Spirit, Creator and Ruler of all. You White people assumed we were savages. You didn't understand. When we sang our praises to the Sun or Moon or Wind, you said we were worshiping idols. Without understanding, you condemned us as lost souls just because our form of worship was different from yours.
>
> We saw the Great Spirit's work in almost everything: Sun, Moon, Stars, Trees, Wind, and Mountains. Sometimes we approached Him through these things. Was that so bad? I think we have a true belief in the Supreme Being, a stronger faith than that of most Whites, who have called us pagans. . . . Indians living close to Nature and Nature's Ruler are not living in darkness.
>
> Did you know that Trees talk? Well, they do. They talk to each other, and they'll talk to you if you listen. Trouble is, most White people don't listen. They never learned to listen to the Indians, so I don't suppose they'll listen to other voices in Nature. But I have learned a lot from trees. Sometimes about the weather, sometimes about the animals, and sometimes about the Great Spirit.

There are even some Native American people today who may criticize me for perpetuating what they consider a romantic stereotype of our tribal heritage, culture, and ideology. But anyone who has spent as much time in Nature as I have, learning from the elders and the Earth, cannot help acquiring a certain amount of romanticism. I grew up the hard way, in poverty and in a broken family; I have lived both on the reservation and in the city. And although the majority of Native American people today are still fighting the forces of genocide, discrimination, unemployment, poverty, alcoholism, poor health, and land-grabbing, many Native Americans are also struggling to bring back their ancient knowledge, beliefs, myths, religious ceremonies, and philosophy. They too are trying to "relearn" about Nature because many of them have lost their bonding with the Earth matrix. They lost this bonding because Western society tried to force Indians into assimilation and because most school systems in the United States, on and off the reservation, do not provide Indian and non-Indian people with an opportunity to study tribal history, heritage and culture, or mythology as part of the regular curriculum.

It has only been during the last decade that Native American people have finally been able to rejuvenate their ancient rituals, ceremonies, and traditional religions without fear of reprimand. Hence we now see many of them returning to the sacred sweat lodge, vision quests, women's Moontime ceremonies, and various sacred dances. The Sun Dances of the Lakota, Cheyenne, Crow, Arapaho, Hidasta/Mandan, and the Blood/Blackfeet people are very difficult, arduous, full of sacrifice and hardship; but there is also a certain degree of "Nature" romanticism associated with them. Some of these tribes are even beginning to let non-Indian people participate in the ancient dances. It is during these times that the ancient myths and esoteric teachings are given to the people while the ceremonial experience itself serves to reestablish one's relationship to Nature, and our great kinship with all life.

Other tribal dances represent myths and stories in a ceremonial way. For example, the sacred White Deerskin Dances of my tribal people is a reenactment of the world's Creation. While the medicine man recites an ancient creation myth, the other Indian people sing and dance with bird feathers, animal hides, animal teeth, flint rocks, and herbs. Participation in ceremony reaffirms a sense that Nature is indeed full of spirits and is indeed spiritual. Bonding processes with the Earth can help us to respect Nature and perhaps become more spiritual in our lives.

On the other hand, I believe that some human beings have become dissociated and calloused toward Nature because they do not have myth, ritual, or some other way to bond with the Earth. I have seen it happen to Native American people who were removed from their land, culture, and religion. People who no longer bond with Nature for whatever reason soon become apathetic and even sometimes antagonistic toward the Earth. Their value systems and ideologies begin to change with respect to life and the world we all live in. The psychologist Carl Jung described the problem this way:

> We distinctly resent the idea of invisible and arbitrary forces, for it is not so long ago that we made our escape from that frightening world of dreams and superstitions, and constructed for ourselves a picture of the cosmos worthy of rational consciousness, that latest and greatest achievement of man. We are now surrounded by a world that is obedient to rational laws. . . . [I]t is civilized man who strives therefore to dominate nature and devotes his greatest efforts to the discovery of natural causes which will give him the key to nature's secret laboratory. That is why he strongly resents the idea of arbitrary powers and denies them. Their existence would amount to proof that his attempt to dominate nature is futile after all.

The differences in worldviews, religious beliefs, and understandings about the significance of myths, and ultimately the conflict of values (spiritual versus economic), can most clearly be seen in the debate over environmental issues. Especially in meetings and legal battles in which traditional Native Americans are trying to convince government officials, land-industrial representatives, and corporate attorneys that a particular site or place should not be exploited, altered, desecrated, or destroyed under the principle of "majority rule," or for the greater good of the greatest number. How can you convince someone who has lived in an artificial world all his or her life that certain parts of Nature and the Earth are sacred? How can you convince those who are in a position of power, authority, and decision-making that sometimes the spiritual and aesthetic value of certain parts of the land is more important than their economic value? Such representatives have never danced barefoot upon the Earth; they have never stood naked and fasting and praying to their Creator, crying for a vision on top of a sacred mountain or inside a cave or sweat lodge. As a result, they have never been provided with an opportunity to "sense" and "feel" the spirits of the Earth.

From their viewpoint, the only valid religious and spiritual experiences are those that are conducted in a church, a man-made, unnatural structure separated from the natural environment. Consequently, some representatives of Western society have no means of grasping the Native American tribal concept of sacred sites and power centers. These ancient power centers and sacred sites are where we, as traditional Native healers, ceremonial leaders, and shamans, go to confirm our knowledge about Nature's language, symbols, and spiritual communications.

Therefore, how can traditional Indians help the representatives of Western society understand the mythic, symbolic, and spiritual significance of religious and mythological sites, which in terms of meaning, purpose, and function goes far beyond the "church" concept and analogy? On a much smaller scale, how can traditional Indians help Western people in general understand why we consider Coyote, Buffalo, Grizzly Bear, Wolf, Eagle, or even Rattlesnake sacred when they have not been taught any kind of ancient myths and Nature stories? I hope that what I have shared here can help with that problem.

Once, during a conflict over the use of, and protection of, ancient ceremonial grounds at Ishi-Pishi Falls, which is considered "the

Center of the World" for the Karuk Indian tribe, I heard a U.S. Forest Service representative from the Six Rivers National Forest in California remark: "I don't understand why you Indians are making such a big deal about fairy tales and fairyland types of places." I read him the following quote by Mircea Eliade, hoping it would bridge the gap:

> In societies where myth is still alive the Natives carefully distinguish myths, "true stories," from fables or tales, which they call "false stories." This distinction made by Natives between "true stories" and "false stories" is significant. Both categories of narratives present "histories," that is, relate a series of events that took place in a distant and fabulous past. Although the actors in myths are usually gods and Supernatural Beings, while those in tales are heroes or miraculous animals, all the actors share the common trait that they do not belong to the everyday world. Nevertheless, the Natives have felt that the two kinds of "stories" are basically different. For everything that the myths relate concerns them directly, while the tales and fables refer to events that, even when they have caused changes in the World, have not altered the human condition.
>
> Myths, that is, narrate not only the origin of the World, of animals, of plants, of birds, and of man, but also all the primordial events in consequence of which man became what he is today: mortal, sexed, organized in a society, obliged to work in order to live, and working in accordance with certain rules. If the World exists, if man exists, it is because Supernatural Beings exercised creative powers in the "Beginning." But after the cosmogony and the creation of man other events occurred, and man as he is today is the direct result of those mythical events, he is constituted by those events.

Ancient myths, legends, and Nature stories are linked to space and time; and space and time become fused into the holy. Though holy or sacred grounds and sites are often defined geographically and culturally, all tribes, all indigenous cultural groups, regardless of their differences or similarities, relate to those phenomena in terms of "power." According to the ancient worldview, everything in Nature is a source

of power, good, bad, or neutral. One must have power in order to survive because we live in a very powerful world, both the past world and
the contemporary world. Most of these powers have existed since the
Beginning of Creation, and despite the encroachment of civilization,
the powers still exist today. Some of the powers are seen and some are
unseen, as in the case of spirits that inhabit different places in Nature,
on the Earth, around the Earth, and in outer space. The powers from
Nature may be demonstrated or perceived for what they really are, in
the form of all those who walk, crawl, fly, and swim—in other words,
what the traditional Indian people call "all our relations." Believing in
this perspective might help make it more real, but such phenomena are
a reality within themselves, whether Western humankind believes in it
or not. Although most people in contemporary society might consider
it foolish to try to communicate with Nature, Nature is constantly
trying to communicate to us.

Some people might try to separate themselves from Nature or
"transcend" Nature mentally, but the mere fact that we are human
beings and part of the great web of life makes us all part of Nature.
We are influenced and affected by Nature, and we in turn directly
influence and affect Nature, positively or negatively. There is no
escaping this relationship even after or beyond death because birth,
growth, old age, and death are all a natural part of the life cycles in
Nature. And power is involved in every cycle, in every season, in
every direction, and in the temporal, spatial, and geographical realms.
Ancient myths and Nature stories help teach us this reality, while
ritual and ceremony provide us with the experiential opportunity to
confirm it.

The ancient myths and Nature stories, therefore, also teach us
about the concept of powers: what they are, where they come
from, what they do, and how to deal with them both past and present.
With such knowledge comes empowerment, higher intelligence, and

spirituality. When we begin to understand this reality, our ideology changes because our relationship to Nature changes, and with that change comes a sense of respect, responsibility, and reciprocity. The concept of conservation and the need to clean up the environment might also bring forth a sense of responsibility to protect and preserve Nature before it becomes totally polluted, altered, or destroyed.

It is essentially with all this in mind that I decided to write this book and share such spiritual knowledge. Learn to love the Earth and care for it, as my ancestors have tried to do and as I have tried to do in carrying on the tradition. Learn to communicate with the spirits of the Earth and you will surely discover that they will communicate in return. And as you begin to learn that Nature is spiritual, you will also begin to learn more about your own spirituality, because all life is in a sacred circle of kinship.

In closing, I would like to leave you with one more ancient story from the Iroquois Six Nations, as told to me by Chief Beeman Logan of the Seneca Nation:

A long, long time ago, there were no stories in the world. Life was not easy for the people, especially during the long winters when the cold wind blew hard and snow was deep.

One winter day a young boy decided to go hunting because his family was low on food. He demonstrated good skills as a hunter and managed to shoot a turkey and a few grouse. The load became heavy as he tried to walk back home, so he grew more and more tired. He decided to rest next to a strange rock that was shaped like a human's head. A few minutes later he heard a voice speak to him, and it scared him.

He thought at first that his tired mind was playing tricks on him. Once again the mysterious voice got louder and said: "Come closer and I will tell you a story." The boy jumped up and looked, but he couldn't see anybody. He called out in fear: "Who are you?"

"I am the Great Stone," said a rumbling voice which seemed to come from somewhere inside the Earth. Then the boy realized it was a big rock next to him that had spoken. So he got the courage to talk to it and said: "If you are really a talking stone, then tell me your story."

The rock replied, "First you must offer me a gift." So the boy took one of the birds he had killed and some tobacco his grandparents had taught him to use for praying, and made an offering. He placed them on the sacred rock.

The Great Stone began to speak. It told a wonderful story of how the Earth was created and the powers were made. As the boy listened, he did not feel the cold wind and snow. After listening carefully, as if trying to memorize the story, he then stood up and thanked the stone. He said: "Thank you, Grandfather. I will go now and share the story with others. But I will come back again tomorrow."

The young hunter hurried home to the longhouse. When he got there he told everyone about his experience and what he had learned. They all gathered around the campfire and listened intently. As the boy talked, a strange thing happened. The story seemed to warm everyone up and drive away the cold and snow. And everyone slept well that night and had good dreams.

The next day the boy hunter was successful in shooting game. He stopped by the Great Stone and shared his game. The stone told him another story and he listened with a sincere heart. It went on like this for a long time, all through the winter season. Each day the young boy shared his tobacco and game birds, and each day in return he received more ancient stories about the "old times." He heard stories of talking animals and monsters, tales of what things were like when the Earth was first created and young. He heard stories about Nature, the Great Spirit, and the powers of Nature. The stories taught him good lessons about life, and about the life around him. And in the traditional Indian way, he always shared his stories with the people so they too could learn and become wise.

One day, near the beginning of spring, the Great Stone told the young hunter: "I have told you all the stories I know in the world. So now they are yours to keep and to teach the people. All I ask in return is that you promise to keep the stories going from one generation until the next. And have the people add more stories to the stories I have shared. In this way everyone will have a chance to learn something."

So this is what came to pass, and this is how it has been for our Native people since the original times. The stories are usually told in the winter, and everyone gets a fair chance to learn, to share, and to pass the knowledge on to the next generation.

SUGGESTED READING

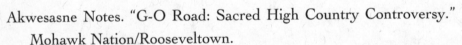

Akwesasne Notes. "G-O Road: Sacred High Country Controversy." Mohawk Nation/Rooseveltown.

Andrade, Roy. *Anthropological Studies of Dreams*. Homewood, Ill.: Dorsey, 1961.

Angulo, Jaime de. *Indian Tales*. New York: Ballantine, 1953.

Barsness, Larry. *Heads, Hides, and Horns: The Complete Buffalo Book*. Ft. Worth, Tex.: Christian University Press, 1985.

Bean, Lowell. "Power and Its Application in Native California." In *Native Californians*, edited by Lowell Bean and Thomas Blackburn. Romano, Calif.: Ballena, 1976.

Bonneyea, Brien. *A Dictionary of Superstitions and Mythology*. London: London Folk Press, 1976.

Boyd, Doug. *Rolling Thunder*. New York: Random House, 1974.

Brown, Joseph E. "The Native Contributions to Science, Engineering, and Medicine." *Science*, 1975.

———. *Animals of the Soul.* Rockport, Mass.: Element, 1992.

Buckley, Thomas. "Monsters and the Quest for Balance in Native Northwest California." In *Manlike Monsters on Trial: Early Records and Modern Evidence*, Michael M. Ames. Vancouver: University of British Columbia Press, 1980.

Campbell, Joseph. *The Hero with a Thousand Faces.* Princeton, N.J.: Princeton University Press, 1968.

Clark, Ella. *Indian Legends of the Pacific Northwest.* Berkeley, Calif.: U.C. Berkeley Press, 1936.

Craven, Margaret. *I Heard the Owl Call My Name.* New York: Dell, 1980.

Dary, David. *The Buffalo Book.* Cleveland: Swallow Press, 1974.

Dixon, R. "Some Shamans of Northern California." *Journal of American Folklore* (Berkeley), 1904.

DuBois, Cora. *Wintun Ethnography. American Archaeology*, 1953.

Eliade, Mircea. *The Myth of the Eternal Return.* Translated by W. Trask. Princeton: Princeton University Press, 1964.

———. *Myths, Rites, and Symbols.* Translated by W. Beane and W. Doty. San Francisco: Harper and Row, 1975.

———. *Shamanism.* New York: Pantheon, 1965.

Emmerson, Ellen. *Indian Myths.* Cambridge, Mass.: Osgood, 1888.

Erdoes, Richard, and John Lame Deer. *Lame Deer Seeker of Visions.* New York: Simon and Schuster, 1972.

Evans-Wentz, W. Y. *Cuchama and the Sacred Mountains.* Cleveland: Swallow, 1989.

Feher-Elston, Catherine. *RavenSong.* Flagstaff: Northland Publishing Co., 1952.

Fire Lame Deer, Archie, and Richard Erdoes. *The Path of Power.* Santa Fe: Bear, 1992.

Fiske, John. "Myths and Myth Makers: Old Tales and Superstitions." *Comparative Mythology Journal* (Boston), 1896.

Fraiberg, Selma. *The Magic Years.* New York: Scribner's, 1968.

Fromm, Erich. *The Forgotten Language: An Introduction to the Understanding of Fairy Tales and Dreams.* New York: Grove Atlantic, 1987.

Garfield, Patricia. *Creative Dreaming.* New York: Ballantine, 1974.

Goodman, Jeffrey. *We Are the Earthquake Generation.* New York: Berkley, 1978.

Halifax, Joan. *Shamanic Voices.* New York: Dutton, 1978.

Harrington, J. P. *Tobacco Among the Karuk Indians.* Berkeley, Calif.: U.C. Berkeley Press, 1938.

Jaimes, Annette. *The State of Native America: Genocide, Colonization, and Resistance.* Boston: South End, 1992.

Jaynes, Julian. *The Origin of Consciousness in the Breakdown of the Bicameral Mind.* New York: Houghton Mifflin, 1977.

Jung, Carl. *Modern Man in Search of a Soul.* New York: Harcourt Brace and World, 1933.

————. *The Four Archetypes: Mother, Spirit, Trickster and Rebirth.* Princeton, N.J.: Princeton University Press, 1959.

Krippner, Stanley, and Alberto Villoldo. *The Realms of Healing.* Milbrae, Calif.: Celestial Arts, 1978.

Kroeber, Alfred L. *Handbook of the Indians of California.* Washington, D.C.: Bureau of Ethnology, 1927.

————. *Yurok Myths.* Berkeley: University of California Press, 1976.

Lake, Robert. *Chilula: People from the Ancient Redwoods.* Lanham, Md.: University Press of America, 1982.

Larson, Stephen. *The Shaman's Doorway.* New York: Harper Colophon, 1976.

Medicine Grizzly Bear; Lake, Robert. *Native Healer.* Wheaton, Ill.: Quest Books/Theosophical Society, 1992.

Nagera, Humberto. "The Imaginary Companion: Its Significance for

Ego Development and Conflict Solution." In *The Psychoanalytic Study of the Child*. New York: International University Press, 1969.

Neihardt, John G. *Black Elk Speaks*. Lincoln: University of Nebraska Press, 1979.

Nicholson, Shirley. *Gaia's Hidden Life: The Unseen Intelligence of Nature*. Wheaton, Ill.: Quest, 1992.

Ornstein, Robert. *The Psychology of Consciousness*. New York: Viking, 1971.

Park, Willard Z. *Shamanism in Western North America*. New York: Bantam, 1938.

Pearce, Joseph. *The Magical Child*. New York: Dutton, 1977.

Pelletier, Kenneth. *Mind as Healer, Mind as Slayer*. New York: Dell, 1977.

Piaget, Jean. *Play, Dreams, and Imitation in Childhood*. New York: Norton, 1962.

Robinson, Herbert. *The Fairylore of Europe: Myths and Legends of All Nations*. London: London, 1930.

Rockwell, David. *Giving Voice to Bear*. New York: Rinehart, 1990.

Sun Bear and Wabun Wind. *Dancing with the Wheel*. New York: Simon and Schuster, 1991.

Swan, James. *The Power of Place*. Wheaton, Ill.: Quest, 1992.

———. *Nature as Teacher and Healer*. New York: Random House, 1993.

Tart, Charles. *Altered States of Consciousness*. New York: John Wiley and Sons, 1969.

Tedlock, Dennis and Barbara. *Teachings from the American Earth*. New York: Liveright, 1975.

Tributsch, Helmut. *When the Snakes Awake: Animals and Earthquake Prediction*. Cambridge, Mass.: MIT Press, 1982.

INDEX

▼▼▼

Index

ABOUT THE AUTHOR

▼▼▼

Bobby Lake-Thom, known as Medicine Grizzly Bear, is a traditional Native healer and spiritual teacher of Karuk and Seneca descent (affiliated with the Quartz Valley Indian Reservation in California). He has been schooled in both Western and Native American traditions and has taught and lectured extensively across the United States for more than three decades. He is the author of two previous books on Native American culture and spirituality, *Native Healer* and *Chilula: People from the Ancient Redwoods*, and his articles have appeared in *The Indian Historian*, *The Journal for Ethnic Studies*, *Quest* magazine, *Shaman's Drum*, and other publications. He lives near Mt. Shasta in Yreka, California.

NOTE

▼▼▼▼▼▼▼▼▼▼▼▼▼▼▼▼▼▼▼▼▼▼▼▼▼▼▼▼▼▼▼▼▼▼▼▼

The elders of our tribe and ceremonial leaders could use your help. They are not supported by government funds or tribal funds; nor are they funded by church-type nonprofit organizational funds. Everything is done on a volunteer and donation basis. And it costs a lot of money and resources to bring the elders together and transport them to gatherings, and to sponsor our sacred dances and rituals. Our few remaining Native healers are unemployed and provide doctoring services to the people on a donation basis only; hence they too do not receive financial support for their spiritual work and often need funds to buy firewood and ceremonial material, or gas money to gather herbs and even to pay their own basic domestic bills.

Thus, if you feel compassion in your heart to help them, please send money donations to the following address (your donation is tax-deductible):

Robert Lake Thom
www.nativehealer.net
760 Marvin Way
Dixon, CA 95620